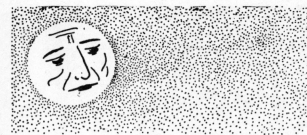

INDIAN SLEEP—MAN TALES

"The moccasins of Po-too Yeo, the Sleep Man, follow the trail of the Evening Star."

Indian
SLEEP-MAN
Tales

By BERNICE G. ANDERSON

ILLUSTRATED BY
SEARS FRANK AND THE AUTHOR

*Authentic legends of the
Otoe Tribe*

GREENWICH HOUSE
Distributed by Crown Publishers, Inc.
New York

Dedicated to ROBERT ARTHUR ANDERSON, *my own paleface son, to whom the Indian, "Sharp Claws," of this story gave the name, "Sayga-pahee nea," meaning "Little Sharp Claws."*

This edition is published by Greenwich House, a division
of Arlington House, Inc., distributed by Crown Publishers,
Inc., by arrangement with The Caxton Printers, Ltd.

Manufactured in the United States of America

LIBRARY OF CONGRESS CATALOGING IN PUBLICATION DATA

Anderson, Bernice G
Indian Sleep-Man tales.

1. Oto Indians—legends. 2. Indians of North America—
Kansas—Legends. I. Title.
E99.087A6   1984   398.2′08997   83-20810
ISBN 0-517-062534

l k j i h

MANY MOONS and many moons ago, as the red man would say, the Otoe tribesmen lived in a huge circle village of tepees on the rolling prairie and low hill country of what is now the state of Nebraska.

On their hunting and fishing trips they roamed all over the plains country, going many, many miles from their home village.

They were happy people because they were free to live as they loved to live. But today the Otoe Indian village is not colorful and exciting, as it used to be. It is merely an uninteresting town of common frame houses surrounded by patches of weedy grass, on a Government reservation at Red Rock, Oklahoma.

The Indians did not want to be "corralled," as Bear Chief Mee-way-seh puts it; the older ones still long for the wide prairies and hills.

Today, only when the tribe holds big celebrations are the people truly happy, for at such times the reservation takes on the glamor of the past, and the Indians

PREFACE

are again the wild, free dwellers of the prairies, dancing and singing and telling the old, old legends, as they used to do.

At such celebrations *tow-wa*, the ball game, is sometimes played to cheer the members of the tribe who have had recent sorrow. Always, the sacred ball stick (painted red) which hung in the head chief's tepee for no one knows how many generations is the leading stick when they start the game with the song:

Ee wah hah-in-yah no no
Ho wah coo-jah hah-in-yah no
Ah-hee-skee-jah hon neah nah wee.

Meaning:

We have it: the stick and the ball.
We have it,
We have it,
Our ball that is played in honor of the sad.

This book gives the story of the origin of the game.

In a grove of fine big oak trees a few miles from the village of Red Rock the Otoe tribe often entertains some other tribe for as long a time as "eight Suns and eight Sleeps" (eight days and eight nights).

Everything is done exactly as it was done long ago.

In this story of Chief Mee-way-seh and his family much has been told about those celebrations in the old days. It is a "really true" story, so far as the characters and many of the incidents are concerned. These legends are the ones which Chief Mee-way-seh, Take-Blanket-Away, told to his four sons. They are the legends which were passed by word of mouth from generation to generation in the Otoe tribe.

PREFACE

Different tribes have a similarity in legends, it is found, and this is quite understandable when one knows that at intertribal celebrations, such as the Otoe-Pawnee celebration related in Chapter 9, the visiting tribesmen taught their songs, games, and stories to their hosts (often by means of the sign language, if they did not understand each other's tongue). After a while no one really knew in which tribe certain stories originated, but they were passed from generation to generation just the same.

The head chief of this tribe is an old man now. He has had a stroke of paralysis and has to spend his days in a wheel chair. But in his faded eyes lurks an ever-ready twinkle, and he likes to dream of those years on the prairie, in the circle village of skin lodges, where he, as head chief of the head clan of the tribe, ruled his people with kindly wisdom.

The four boys of the story, Sunlight, Spotted Tail, Surprise, and Sharp Claws [these are their true names], are grown men now, living with their families on the Otoe Reservation. They have taken up many of the ways of the white man, but they still like to don their fringed buckskin trousers and beaded vests, their long headdresses of eagle feathers, and their beaded moccasins, to sing and tell legends in the Otoe tongue, and dance the tribal dances, for they, too, remember the days on the prairie when they were small boys.

Chief Mee-way-seh is the last *active* head chief of the Otoe tribe. At his death Sunlight, his oldest son, will become head chief—but only in name. The glamorous tribal days are gone.

When Sunlight becomes head chief Sharp Claws, the youngest, will move up to position of fourth chief. Each clan has but four chiefs, four being one of the sacred numbers to Indians because the Great Spirit gave us four directions—north, south, east, and west, and four seasons—The Green Moons, The Warm Moons, The Season When the Leaves Put on Their War Paint, and The Snow Season.

Even the Pipe of Peace has, at last, been sold, but only because the tribe has become so poor the members needed the two hundred and fifty dollars which the sale brought.

This act nearly broke the old chief's heart, when, after a council which resembled the old-time meetings around council fires on the Plains, the tribe decided to make the sale. It was indeed a matter of importance, for the Peace Pipe was the tribe's "Secret to happiness," its "Good heart maker," and had been guarded day and night, in the old days, by the Pipe Man, in the head chief's tepee.

In recent years, when white men tried time after time to induce the old chief to sell the pipe, Chief Mee-way-seh protected it from theft in this manner: He appointed one man of the tribe to hide the bowl and another man to hide the stem. Only he knew who the men were, and only the men themselves knew where they had hidden the parts.

My own family and a friend and I have been invited to be the only white guests at many powwows of this tribe, and of the Kaw tribe. We have also visited among other tribes.

PREFACE

Upon one occasion Chief Mee-way-seh honored me by giving me an Indian name. He said, "I name you '*Whoo-graay-do-weh-meh*,' meaning 'Homemaker.'" His son Sharp Claws gave me the sacred red ball stick which hung in the tepee of the head chief of the tribe for no one knows how long. I have it with the understanding that when the tribesmen wish to play the game (which is not often, any more) I am to lend it to them.

To the young palefaces who read this book I give the benediction which Coming Daylight of my story offered in parting: "May the Great Spirit bring sunrise to your hearts!"

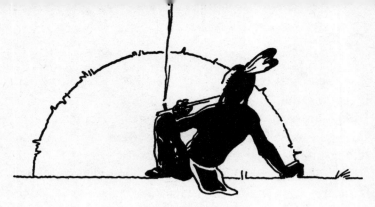

CONTENTS

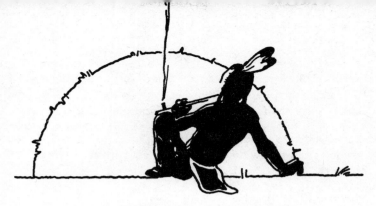

LIST OF ILLUSTRATIONS

LIST OF ILLUSTRATIONS

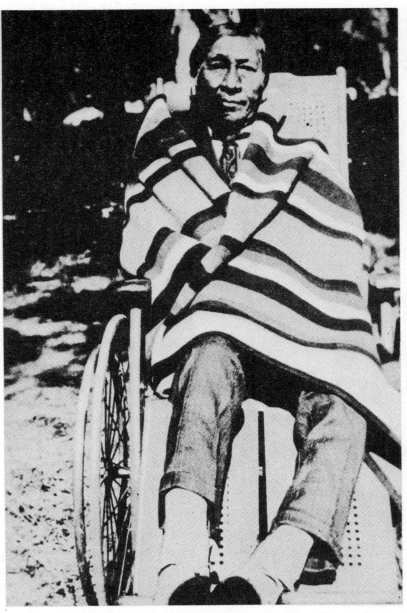

Chief Take-Blanket-Away, last active head chief of Otoe tribe, as he is today.

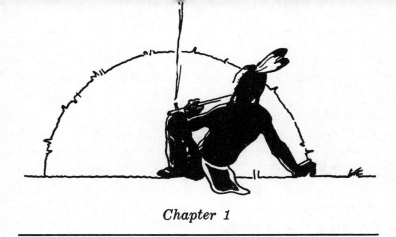

Chapter 1

"HOW" STORIES

"*Yah-wah shee-geh!*" A voice, as clear-toned as the village announcer's bell, sounded from the head chief's painted tepee.

"*Yah-wah shee-geh!*" The voice ascended musically; and this time Circling Eagle, the slim wife of Chief Take-Blanket-Away, stood in the doorway of the tepee, the fringes of her white doeskin dress skipping in the wind, her long, braided black hair blowing back from her shoulders.

The wind sang in a baritone voice. A red leaf scuttled to the ground.

As the woman stepped outside to call again, the rows of shining white elk teeth and tiny painted shells ornamenting her dress chimed rhythmically. The music of her voice, the music of the wind, the music of the chiming ornaments, blended in autumn harmony.

"The Cold Maker will bring the Snow Season to our village before many Sleeps," Circling Eagle remarked to the Pipe Man, who had lifted the flap of the tepee to look out. "Todja-Omayda, the north wind, is announcing it this very dusk hour."

Quickly she moved toward the fire which the bellows of the wind had fanned into life. As she did so her beaded headband and her strings of beads and metal bracelets snatched the reflection of the flames and changed her into a Fire Princess there in the autumn dusk. Or so the Pipe Man thought, as he looked at her.

"*Yah-wah shee-geh!*" Circling Eagle called again, and this time her voice reached the ears of four shouting, scrambling boys who were playing the game of "Coyote-in-the-ring" with other boys of the Otoe village.

Sunlight, the eldest son of Circling Eagle and Chief Take-Blanket-Away was in the act of beating the howling "coyote" with a stick, but he paused for a moment, the stick uplifted, to wave a signal to his mother.

As soon as he could attract their attention he motioned to Spotted Tail and Surprise and Sharp Claws to start with him toward their tepee.

Surprise, who happened to be the "coyote" receiving the beating, was ready to quit, but the other boys were reluctant to leave the game.

The four brothers knew that "*Yah-wah shee-geh*" meant "Someone is coming," and that this mysterious someone was no other than Po-too Yeo, the Sleep Man. They might have been tempted to ignore their mother's summons had they not known that storytelling time always preceded the arrival of this otherwise unwelcome person; but with a boisterous "Good sleep!" to playmates who were already starting toward their own

lodges the *"Skah-cheh-leh"* [game] was ended for that
evening.

In the exact center of the circle village facing the
Place of the Sunrise, the head chief's tepee stood like a
blanketed giant chief, its scarlet and blue and bright
yellow painted symbols dimmed by nightfall.

Circling Eagle was replenishing the lodge fire when
her sons came running in.

A gray banner of smoke sought the outlet at the
peak of the lodge; and as the flames set the rhythm four
wild shadows danced upon the walls.

"Look!" Spotted Tail shouted. "The Shadow Dance
has begun!"

The boys gave a war whoop and at once began to
cause their shadows to perform grotesque antics.

"Yah-wah shee-geh!" Circling Eagle reminded
them as she seated herself beside the fire and took up
her basketry. "The Sleep Man will put you to sleep
standing up; and how will you like that?"

The boys settled, at once, beside the fire and turned
expectant faces toward their tall chieftain father.

"What is the first story to be?" asked Sharp
Claws, ever the most eager of the boys to hear what
he always called the "How" stories.

Laying aside his dyes made from sumac and blue-
berries and colored soil with which he had been painting symbols of the Bear clan upon the tepee walls, Chief
Take-Blanket-Away filled his long pipe with tobacco
from the little beaded sack at his belt. He stood smiling
down upon his youngest son.

Sharp Claws looked up at him and returned the

"Look! The Shadow Dance has begun!"

smile shyly. "Tell us how Mah-sjeem nea, the little white rabbit, got his pink eyes, won't you?" he urged almost in a whisper, for he stood in some awe of this father who knew so many things and who looked so magnificent, on special occasions, in his beaded garments and long feathered war bonnet.

The big chief of the Bear clan puffed long puffs on his pipe. He stood listening for a moment to the small sounds of the night—the sleep tune of the cricket, the shivery voice of Ma-coe-gee, the screech owl, the lullaby croon of the little stream where a bullfrog twanged at the rising moon—while shaggy darkness stole, catlike, around the tepee and crept inside to lie in the far corners where the firelight had failed to reach. Then he seated himself at the opposite side of the fire.

"Ho!" he began. "So you want to hear again how Mah-sjeem nea, the little white rabbit, got his pink eyes, do you? Well, then——"

Many moons and many moons ago a little white rabbit lived in the woods with his grandmother rabbit.

One sun, while the grandmother was in her garden gathering cabbage and carrots and turnips for the noon meal, Mah-sjeem nea ran away.

He ran far into the woods where the shadows made a blue and purple jungle and where the treetops gave queer, whispering noises.

At first these sounds frightened the little white rabbit, and in order to escape them he sped along as briskly as a tumbleweed can travel across our wide prairie in front of the wind.

But the deeper he went into the woods the more whisperings he heard. The more whisperings he heard the more briskly he ran!

But the deeper he went into the woods the more whisperings he heard.

Finally a few words caught his attention and he paused to listen.

"He is a swift runner, that rabbit!" came a distinct voice from the strongest oak tree.

"He is, indeed," replied the chief of the hackberry trees.

"Hoh," thought Mah-sjeem nea, and he bellowed his chest. "So that is what they have been saying! I might have known it all along!"

After that he ran on hurricane feet.

"Hoh!" he said again. "This is easy. Perhaps I can outrun Chief One Eye!"

One Eye was the head chief of the tribe of white rabbits. His record as a runner had never yet been broken.

The vain little white rabbit decided to try to fool his grandmother, for he knew that she had always wanted him to pattern his life after the life of this great chief. When he neared a wild-plum thicket he plucked out one of his eyes as if he were plucking a wild plum. Then he hid it in the thicket and ran to his grandmother's garden.

He entered like a tornado. His grandmother screeched in that high-pitched voice rabbits have and started to run; but when she saw his one eye she wheeled about and bowed very low. She addressed him as "Chief One Eye"; and Mah-sjeem nea bellowed his chest again. He chatted awhile with his grandmother rabbit and tried not to smile over the trick he was playing upon her.

When he had loped back to the wild-plum thicket and had put his eye back into its socket he returned, very leisurely, to his grandmother's garden, and listened to the old rabbit's account of the supposed visit of swift Chief One Eye.

The little fellow was so elated over the success of his trick that he could not resist the fun of trying it again the next day.

While his grandmother was in her garden gathering cabbage and carrots and turnips for the noon meal, he again loped out to the wild-plum thicket, and after plucking out his eye as if he were plucking a wild plum, he hid it in the thicket and ran swiftly, and ever more swiftly, to his grandmother's garden.

The grandmother rabbit felt honored at receiving a second visit from the rabbit whom she thought was the one-eyed chief, and she humbly offered him a bowl of crushed ripe berries to eat.

The berries tasted so delicious, and Mah-sjeem nea was having such fun that he remained longer than he realized; and when he returned to the wild-plum thicket to replace his eye he found that he had left it out so long it had become cold. Pains like thorn pricks stabbed him after he had put the eye back into its socket. He rubbed it with his paws, but this served only to make the pain greater.

The little white rabbit ran whimpering back to his grandmother. His head throbbed, and a throb was in his voice as he begged her to put a poultice of herbs upon his eye.

"Dear, dear! How very pink your eye is!" the grandmother rabbit exclaimed while she did all she could to relieve the pain. "If your grandfather were only here he could make this eye well with his magic, for he was a medicine man of great power."

But the grandfather had been in the Happy Hunting Ground, the Land of the Spirits, for many moons and many moons, and so he could not help his little grandson.

The herb poultice which the grandmother applied took away the pain, but the pink color remained, and the other eye turned pink to match it.

That is how the first white rabbit got its pink eyes. All of his descendants have had pink eyes, too, as you know.

Chief Take-Blanket-Away paused at the end of the story. He looked down at his four deep-breathing sons beside the fire, and turned to smile into the eyes of his wife.

The eyelids of their sons were closed; but Sharp Claws sat up when he felt his father's scrutiny.

"One more story, please, Father!" he begged.

"So you were not asleep, then, my youngest brave?"

"No, Father, and I would like to hear the story of how O-don-bah-shee, the bobcat, lost his tail!"

"That one is too long for tonight, Sharp Claws, but I will tell you a shorter one, if you like, and save the one about O-don-bah-shee until another time."

"All right," Sharp Claws agreed, for young Indians never wheedle nor tease their parents. "Please tell me how you won the name 'Take-Blanket-Away.' "

Chief Take-Blanket-Away smiled again. "You are a true chieftain of tomorrow, my son," he said. "You must always know *how* and *why*. Very well, then, I will tell you:

"When I was thigh high to a buffalo it was the custom of our people to take blankets away from other members of the tribe, if we admired the blankets, and wanted them—and were strong enough to get them.

"We never sneaked into the lodge of another tribesman and stole anything, but if we could get it by giving the other a chance to protect his property we considered it a fair way to do.

"One day I saw a beautiful blanket. It had a background like new-laid snow. The white was interwoven with symbols in the scarlet and russet and gold of autumn leaves, and the blue of summer skies.

"That this blanket was upon the back of one of the strongest braves of the Otoe tribe did not bother me at all. I just took it away from him.

"After that I was called 'Mee-way-seh,' 'Take-Blanket-Away.' "

The eyes of Sharp Claws were two black onyx beads in the firelight. "You were very brave, Father. And how did my mother get her name?"

"You have seen a bird with great wings wheeling round and round in the sky, have you not?"

"Oh, yes! That is the eagle."

"Yes. When your mother was thigh high to an antelope she liked to stand watching the eagle as long as she could see it. Because of this trait she was called 'Way-wee-kay-mee,' 'Circling Eagle.' Is it not a beautiful name?"

"It is. And my own name, Father. Please tell me how I got my name, and then I will go to sleep."

"The Sleep Man may overcome you before I am through!"

"Then I shall ask you again tomorrow night. But please try me, anyway. I am sure I can keep awake!"

"Your name is a Bear clan name, and so is the name 'Spotted-tail!' " began the chief. "You were named for your uncle—my brother, a mighty hunter.

"He was the third chief of the Bear clan, of which I was second until the death of your grandfather, when I became head chief in his place and your uncle became second chief.

"Because he was a chief of the Bear clan he desired a fine necklace of bear claws to wear about his neck. Such a necklace, as you know, distinguishes a Bear chief from the chiefs of the six other clans of our tribe.

"Finally, after studying the stars for many nights, he decided that the sign was right for him to go on this particular bear hunt.

"It was during the Snow Season, but he knew that not all the bears were wintering in their dens, so he started out, going always against the wind, so that Moon-jah, the black bear, could not get his scent.

"If there were the least stir of air and he could not determine from which direction it came, he would wet his finger and hold it up. The side which dried first told him what he needed to know. For a stir of air will carry human scents to warn wild animals of the approach of danger.

"Your uncle went far up into the hills where the trails were smooth with new-laid snow. He killed two black bears; but he had a fight with the last one, and the she-bear dug her sharp claws into his flesh. He wears the scars to this day.

"That is how he won the name 'Sharp Claws.' You were named for him because you were always happy when he allowed you to play with his necklace of bear claws when you were a papoose thigh high to a coyote. You liked his necklace better than mine because of the extra large and particularly sharp set of claws in the center."

Young Sharp Claws, whose eyelids had been growing heavier and heavier, roused himself at the end of the story and murmured, "Sharp—claws—big— sharp——"

But the Sleep Man had overcome him at last, and he left his sentence unfinished.

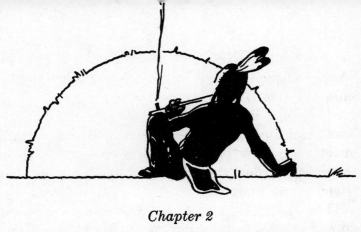

Chapter 2

MORE "HOW" STORIES

THE TWILIGHT GAMES of the Otoe children were ended this evening earlier than usual, and the four sons of the head chief were sitting on the ground in front of their father's tepee.

"See that group of seven stars?" Surprise pointed at the Big Dipper. "Father told me that they represent the seven clans of our tribe."

"Yes, I know," said Sunlight. "And I can pick out the great Bear chief. Can you?"

"There he is, at the head of the group!" Spotted Tail exclaimed. "He is leading the other chiefs. Following him are the Beaver, the Elk, the Coyote, the Eagle, the Buffalo, and the Snake chiefs."

"I see another bright star standing off by itself like our village sentinel," said Sharp Claws.

"That is the Evening Star. Mother says it shows the Sleep Man where to find us," Sunlight remarked.

"And that smoky white trail clear across the sky is called the Dust Trail."

"You are right, my son." Chief Take-Blanket-Away had been standing for some time, unobserved, in the doorway of the lodge. "I am pleased that you remember so accurately these things which I tell you from time to time."

The boys joyfully made room for their father and crowded close against his knees when he seated himself among them.

"Father," Sharp Claws pointed to what the paleface people call "The Milky Way." "How did that trail of dust get into the sky?"

"You are calling for another 'How' story, aren't you, my most inquisitive brave?" smiled the chief.

⊜

Many moons and many moons ago, in what we call the Far Back Times When Animals Could Talk, all the wild animals of the forest and prairie, and all the fowls of the air held a council.

They built a big council fire, and when the flames were savage, like braves giving a war dance, the animals seated themselves in a circle about the fire to decide which, of all present, could make the greatest speed in travel.

After puffing at his long pipe for many breaths the fox arose.

The night was so still that if one of the birds had dropped a feather each one of those strange creatures sitting about the fire would have declared a tree had fallen.

"I can run so swiftly," announced the fox, "that every shrub and all the wild flowers I pass on my journeys bow down thinking I am their ruler, the wind. I can travel so swiftly that the wind himself goes to his lodge behind the heavens for rest when he knows I am traveling about!"

After puffing at his long pipe for many breaths the eagle arose. "I can travel so swiftly," he said, "that I keep the wind under my wings as I beat a pathway across the sky. He cannot escape me. Then I *am* the wind."

After that all the beasts of the forest and prairie and all the fowls of the air began to talk at once. They wrangled until the air was quivering with their clamor, and no one heard what another was saying.

Finally, when the council fire had burned to a sickly reddish-yellow and everyone else was worn out with talking, Shoo-nea, the wild horse, and Chaay-gee, the bison, began the argument all over again.

"My hoofs are the fleetest of the fleet!" the bison bellowed, and his voice made the grass blades tremble.

"My hoofs are even more fleet than that!" whinnied the horse. "And when I run my mane is more beautiful than yours, for it ripples like prairie grass in the wind."

"When *I* run," the bison retorted, "I travel so swiftly no one can see whether my mane ripples or not."

On and on they wrangled until the Bear, chief over all the clans of wild animals, decreed that the two should run a race to settle the matter.

The next night, when all the world was brimming

with moonlight and every tree was splashed with silver, the animals of the forest and prairie and the fowls of the air stood about to witness the race. The air was tense with excitement.

At first the bison took the lead. He lowered his ponderous horns and bellowed like a thousand bullfrogs as he ran. He blinded the horse with the dust storms stirred high by his thudding hoofs.

By midnight Shoo-nea was gaining on him.

With wide, rigid nostrils and flamelit eyes the little wild horse galloped nearer and nearer. His wind-flung mane and tail resembled wings. The sweat on his body was like dripping silver in the moonlight.

The onlookers could scarcely see or breathe because of the white-gray dust which lay like smoke along the

Now the racers were running neck to neck. . . .

trail, but they strained forward, running along the sides of the trail which had been designated as the race track.

Now the racers were running neck to neck. Now Shoo-nea was his body's length ahead of Chaay-gee. The goal was in sight. With a last straining of the muscles the little horse won the race, while the on-lookers barked and howled and twittered at the peaks of their voices. They would have done it for the winner in either case.

Today we Indians consider the horse the swiftest and most beautiful of all animals, and it has become our friend and helper.

The smokelike dust which the racers stirred up went into the sky and remained there just as many other things leave trails to mark their deeds—good or evil—as you young braves will learn.

"*Yah-wah shee-geh!*" called Circling Eagle from within the lodge.

"That Sleep Man comes too early!" Spotted Tail complained.

"Yes, but his coming always brings storytelling time," Sunlight reminded him, "and Father has prom-ised to tell us the story of how O-don-bah-shee, the bob-cat, lost his tail." But he lingered alone for a few minutes after his brothers had started in. "The moc-casins of Po-too Yeo follow the trail of the Evening Star," he murmured, as he stared at the star-flecked sky. "I'd like to catch sight of him!"

The boys entered the lodge and lay down by the fire among their warm robes of buffalo hide.

After watching Chief Take-Blanket-Away puff solemnly at his pipe while the silence of the prairie night arose like a prayer to the Great Spirit, their patience was rewarded by the telling of their favorite story, "How the bobcat lost his tail."

It was a late autumn morning in the Moon When the Wild Geese Fly South. The Cold Maker had blown his breath upon the earth and the green things had turned brown. Each morning and evening the mouths of all the little streams were puckered with ice, though they thawed again during the afternoon, and food was harder to find than it had been during the Warm Moons.

O-don-bah-shee, the bobcat, came out of his den in a hollow tree. His stomach was as empty as that basket your mother is making; and so he went in search of a good place to fish.

He had gone but a short distance when he met Toe-shee-yea, the mink, who was carrying to his own den a big mess of catfish and carp.

The bobcat's mouth dripped water. "Where did you get your nice mess of fish?" he wanted to know.

"In yonder creek," replied the mink, and he went on toward his den.

"Tell me how you managed to catch so many!" O-don-bah-shee implored him. "Please tell me so that I can do likewise!"

"The ice has thawed now," Toe-shee-yea told him,

"and so, if you will sit by the creek and hang your tail in the water the fish will get upon it and nibble at it. You can tell by the number of nibbles you feel when there are a great many fish on your tail; then if you will draw it out very quickly you will find you will have a fine mess for your supper this evening."

"A most excellent idea!" the bobcat replied, and he hurried down to the creek.

All day he sat on the brink of the stream and let his tail hang in the water. His stomach snarled because of its emptiness, and he kept picturing himself with a great feast of fish before him. But, although he often felt nibbles on his tail he did not want to draw it out until he was sure he would have a nice mess of fish upon it.

Toward evening his tail began to hurt. But he thought, "Now I am getting more and more nibbles! What a supper I shall have! What a supper!"

The air became brittle with cold. His teeth began to click together as his whole body shivered, but the greedy fellow waited for more and more nibbles before drawing his tail out of the water.

By sundown sharp pains like arrow pricks were jabbing in and out all along his tail. But he only smacked his big lips and thought again of the supper he expected to have.

At last he could endure the pain no longer. He decided to jerk his tail out very quickly, as the mink had instructed him.

But when he attempted to do so he found that his tail was held fast by some unknown thing!

He pulled and pulled; but alas for the poor bobcat
—*his tail was frozen in the ice!*

"Oh, what an awful fix I'm in!" he lamented, and
at the same time he gave a vicious jerk which pulled
his tail right off!

Poor O-don-bah-shee went toward his den feeling
very empty and very, very angry. And there was a
terrible ache where his tail had been.

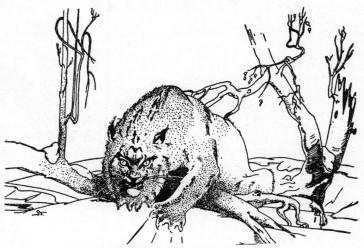

The yellow fire in his eyes burned savagely.

The yellow fire in his eyes burned savagely. As he
slunk along the trail he pounced upon every stray bird
and small animal he could find.

That is the story about how O-don-bah-shee, the
bobcat, lost his tail—and won his name.

He is still looking for that mink, to make him pay
for the mean trick he played.

"I like that story best of all," said Surprise.

"Now it is time for sleep," said their father, "and tomorrow night you shall have another story."

Soon the lodge was quiet except for the deep breathing of the four boys, and the chief and his wife who lay, like their sons, with their feet toward the fire.

Outside the tepee the noiseless gliding of the stars went on toward the western rim of the prairie, while coyotes howled at the shadows on the moon.

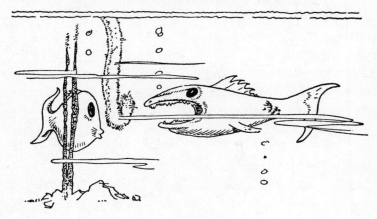

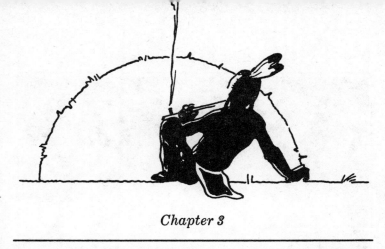

Chapter 3

HOW THE SNOW BUNTING EARNED ITS NAME

THE SNOW SEASON was proving to be a very icy one.
More buffalo robes were brought into use, and bigger
fires warmed the lodges of the tribesmen.

The people were glad that they had their winter
wigwams in which to spend the cold months. Sunlight,
Spotted Tail, Surprise, and Sharp Claws themselves
had helped build a new wigwam for their family this
season. They had cut the saplings along the creek and
had helped apply the clay and sod over the domelike
framework which the bent saplings formed. And they
had helped make the clay and sod secure by means of
small pliant twigs.

Now that the winter was here the boys often heated
smooth, round stones in their fire and, after wrapping
them in strips of worn blankets, they hugged them
close to their bodies after they crawled into their piles
of heavy robes for the night.

Tonight new snow was falling in big, soft petals

New snow was falling in big, soft petals as from some forgotten wild-plum tree.

as from some forgotten wild-plum tree. They clung to the wigwams, making them look like huddled ghosts.

"Tell us a snow story tonight, will you, Father?" begged Sharp Claws as the chief was fastening the flap of the door more securely against the prowling cold.

"Yes. The one about the Bird of Snow," Spotted Tail added, with eagerness.

The chief stretched his moccasined feet toward the fire and began his story.

In the Far Back Times When Animals Could Talk, Wacunda, the Great Spirit, sent word to the birds and animals of the Snow Season that He was planning to make them a visit. The Spirit Runner who brought the message said that Wacunda would tarry only where He might find a camping ground of smooth clean snow kept in readiness for him.

On a snow-spread hillside the birds and animals of the Snow Season built a council fire; and after the flames were leaping high, in an attempt to meet the millions of tiny council fires in the far sky, a plain little bird without a name arose from the circle.

"I know of a place on the prairie where the snow is fresh and clean and smooth," he said.

"I know of such a place, too," said another plain little bird without a name. "When daylight returns I can easily find it."

The morning came, at last. By this time the council fire was but ashes.

On a snow-spread hillside the birds and animals of the Snow Season built a council fire.

"Now show us this place," a red fox demanded; and he hid a smile behind his paw.

"Then follow my flight," replied the plain little bird without a name, and he mounted the sky, trailed by his brother birds.

The animals left the council fire and loped along the crusty white prairie trails, while they kept their eyes upon the tracery of wings against the sky.

But when the fox saw the birds sinking lower and lower toward a smooth hollow between two knolls his grin ran out at the corners of his mouth like the juice of crushed berries, and he made a sudden dash into the very heart of the hollow.

All the animals gasped in surprise. But they soon understood that the fox was having another of his little jokes, and so they made the air brittle with their laughter.

The plain little birds without a name were heavy of heart—so heavy that they could not immediately rise again. For only happy hearts can mount the skies. They sank down upon the trampled snow.

"Let us return to our council fire," said the mischief maker, "and decide where next to look for a place where the snow is fresh and clean and smooth," and his laughter echoed over the knolls and hollows as he led the other animals back to the fire.

But the birds did not attempt to follow. After they had sat awhile quivering unhappily in the snow their head chief stood up.

"I know of another hollow as smooth and as clean

as this one was. Let us fly to it and protect it with our breasts until Wacunda shall come to us," he said.

And so the hearts of the bird tribe became light again, and they sang to the sky as they arose.

This time they did not tell the animals to follow their flight. They went secretly; and their prayers ascended to the Great Spirit as their wings flickered sharply against the doors of the heavens.

Having found the hollow of clean smooth snow, they saw that the white crust would hold up their tiny bodies without receiving the slightest mar. And so the tribe of plain little birds without a name settled lightly down upon the surface to protect its beauty with their soft breasts. They did not mind the cold. They cared only for the coming of Wacunda.

As night dropped a purple blanket over the sleeping plains the little birds longed to seek a safe tree in which to sleep, but they dared not leave the smooth clean hollow lest the naughty fox should come along and trample its surface. They would not have time to find another place before the Great Spirit should come.

At midnight, when the world was as black as the black dyes in your mother's color pots, and the snow was the only whiteness anywhere—except the stars—the birds awoke suddenly, as one bird, jerking their fuzzy heads out from beneath their wings.

Why were those hundreds of lights circling about them? Had the stars come down from the sky to serve as tiny campfires to warm their shivering bodies?

No! The lights were only reflections of the stars, in wild animals' eyes! The animals who had once been

their friends were now their tormentors! They had
hunted until they had found them, and were now going
to drive them from the place they had been keeping
spotless for the coming of the Great Spirit.

The birds trembled. But like braves on the warpath they would not show their fear.

Suddenly, out of the stillness, the voice of Wacunda
came like the hissing of an arrow:

"Go, thoughtless beasts! I come only to visit these
who have kept in readiness a camping ground of
smooth clean snow. For the snow is like living hearts.
Only untrampled snow is clean enough to receive the
visits of the Great Spirit!"

The animals hung their heads so low their noses
plowed the snow as they slunk away. But the birds
mounted on happy wings, alighting upon the shoulders
and outstretched hands of the Great Spirit. And Wacunda put songs into their throats.

Snow clung to the breasts and flecked the wings
and heads of the plain little birds without a name.

"You are plain birds no longer," said Wacunda,
with a smile that warmed the place like summer. "For
the snow shall remain where it clings. And let no one
say that you are birds without a name, for from now
on your names shall be Bird of Snow, because your
hearts were ready to receive the Great Spirit."

That is how the Bird of Snow (Snow Bunting)
earned its name.

After Chief Take-Blanket-Away had finished telling the story the little family sat in silence, listening

to the footsteps of the snow as it tiptoed down, apparently wishing not to disturb the peace of the ghost-like village.

And although the Sleep Man made his usual visit to every Otoe lodge he left no footprints as he came and departed in the white night.

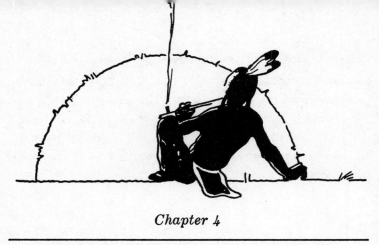

Chapter 4

HOW THE MAN GOT INTO THE MOON

"Yes, you can see him if you look sharply," Chief Take-Blanket-Away told his sons.

The nights were warmer again, and the boys were about to hear the first Sleep Man tale of the evening as they stood outside the door of their lodge. Spotted Tail had pointed to the Man in the Moon with the exclamation, "I see him, I see him!"

"How did he get away up there, Father?" Sharp Claws inquired eagerly.

"He jumped up there to hide," answered the chief.

Once in the far-back times, when this Man in the Moon was a little boy thigh high to a buffalo, he lived with his grandmother in a faraway circle village.

When this boy, Running Antelope, was tall like a straight young sapling, and, like the sapling had learned the ways of life's sun and wind, his tribesmen

came from the faraway village to visit at the prairie
village of a harsh, unkind chief.

There have been but few unkind chiefs in the his-
tory of the red man's world, but each bad chief has
met with punishment in one way or another.

Among the villagers was a young woman who wore
a dress of doeskin whitened with clay and trimmed
with the milk teeth of elks and with tips of turkey
feathers, and porcupine quills. The perfume of burned
sweetgrass, for which she had traded with other tribes
from afar off toward the sunset, clung to her hair.
Upon her arms bracelets of turquoise and silver jan-
gled strange music.

When Running Antelope learned that her name
was Little Hill he decided the name was fitting, for her
face made him think of the sunrise upon a hillcrest,
and her voice was like the singing of wind on a hill.

After the days of celebration were over, he came
to the young woman and wrapped her in his marriage
blanket, and together they set up a home in the village
of Little Hill's tribesmen.

Long days of the Green Moons were spent in the
building of a tepee and the painting of symbols of the
sun, the new moon, the bear, the eagle, on the walls of
dressed skin.

Little Hill cooked the meals, tanned the hides, made
pottery out of red and white clay. And as she worked
Running Antelope sang his own tribal songs to her
while the air became scented with the perfume of
burning sweetgrass upon the embers of the lodge fire.

Running Antelope's songs were wistful with mention of mountains, spicy with the breath of the pines; he sang of the bluebells and wild heliotrope; of clematis, called Ghosts' Lariat; he sang of the horned lark, called Little Black Breast; of the chinook winds that he called Good Old Man. And Little Hill smiled as she worked.

Every night the people of the prairie tribe gathered around a leaping fire near the center of the village. Some of the younger ones danced and sang, while others played tomtoms, and the old men storytellers told the familiar legends of the tribe. Later, the harsh, unkind chief came from his tepee and threw coral and turquoise and bright metal beads upon the ground for his people to gather for their own. He thought that in this way he could get his tribesmen to love him. But love is won only through *love*.

One night, when the moon was lifting its flame-colored disk over the rim of the prairie and the songs of the tribesmen were crowding the air above the village bonfire, Running Antelope carried a pouchful of beads home to Little Hill, who had preferred to spend the evening alone in their lodge.

But when he lifted the door flap the quiet of the tepee met him and silenced the pleasantry that lay upon his lips. No look as of the sunrise upon a hillcrest met his eyes; no voice like the singing of wind on a hill came to his ears. His lodge fire was gray.

The young man ran back to the village bonfire and searched the faces of the singers around the big drums; he searched the faces of the dancers where light and shadow flickered as they moved; he hunted among the people who were still fingering the dust in search of beads which might be hidden there. But nowhere in that noise-filled circle of light could his wife be found.

Then darkness filled the heart of Running Antelope, for he remembered that the cruel chief had threatened to steal Little Hill and take her to his own lodge.

Creepingly, as went the padded footsteps of the panther, the young man's moccasined feet sought the shadowed side of the head chief's tepee. He listened for the sound of voices within the lodge. His heart thudded with such resounding that he wondered it did not shake the tepee as the wind was shaking the cottonwood tree behind him.

Then came the singing of wind on a hillcrest, and he knew that his wife was in the lodge of the head chief, for no other voice could bring such music to his ears.

He no longer crept with the padded footsteps of the panther, but with a panther's cry and a panther's spring he found himself facing the head chief of his tribe.

Little Hill gave an answering cry as of a panther for its mate, but the chief would not let her go to her husband. He ordered Running Antelope out of his lodge.

Running Antelope made another panther spring at the chief, but the chief was ready with his sharpened hunting knife and his poisoned arrows, and the young man was forced to run to save his life.

The chief pursued him. They ran many, many steps along shadowy trails, leaping over stone-crested knolls, stumbling into buffalo wallows, and tripping over cactus with a thousand arrow points in it.

They came to a pool of water flowered with stars. The chief was almost upon Running Antelope, when the young man called upon the Water Spirits to save him.

...he felt himself being whisked up into the sky.

Then suddenly he felt himself being whisked up into the sky by a great spout of water.

At sight of the water spout the chief covered his face. "A spirit dances before me," he cried, "and I dare not look upon it or I die!"

When he looked up again Running Antelope was nowhere in sight. The Water Spirits had taken him to the moon to live.

"That is he whom we see looking down at us."

That is he whom we see looking down at us. He is wondering if Little Hill misses him, and if the cruel chief is still looking for him.

He does not know that one night—still in the far-back times—the old chief, upon seeing the reflection of the young man's face upon the moonlit pool, rushed into the deep water and was drowned by the Water Spirits.

The old chief rushed into the deep water and was drowned by the Water Spirits.

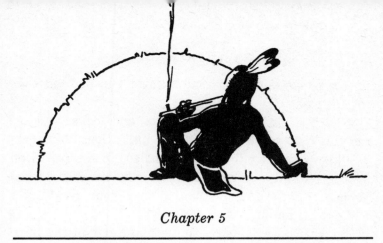

Chapter 5

TOW-WA, THE BALL GAME

THE SPRING MOONS had come again.

The chief of the Elk clan, as directed by Chief Take-Blanket-Away, had given instructions to the villagers to plant their corn and to cultivate it. They had had corn dances and feasts celebrating the planting season, and they had prayed to the Great Spirit their tribal prayer:

> Give us strength, Wacunda,
> That we may live to another day
> Of growing crops!

It was a rich season of prayer and song worship.

On a bright afternoon Sharp Claws had wandered many steps from the circle camp of tepees facing the Place of the Rising Sun. He was gathering wind anemones and other wild flowers for his mother, and had stopped to watch a bird as it idled cloud-high against the deep blue of the sky, when upon looking down again, he saw a man kneeling beside a clear, sun-painted pool not far away.

Sharp Claws squinted his eyes and looked again; and this time he saw that it was his father.

"Come, my son," the chief called, in a voice that always reminded Sharp Claws of wind in the cedars, "come, kneel here beside me and close your eyes!" He held out his hand.

Sharp Claws came on tiptoe and knelt in the lush grass rimming the pool.

"Listen!" commanded his father softly. "Be still, and listen with the ears of your heart."

The breathing of the wind came through the tall grass; no other sound broke the prairie's stillness.

"Are you hearing the voice of the Great Spirit, my son?"

"Yes, Father."

"You can hear it upon the wind, but only when your mind is still and your heart listens!"

The boy nodded without speaking.

"Now, open your eyes and look into the face of Wacunda in this calm pool!" Chief Take-Blanket-Away directed, still in that voice of wind in the cedars. "Look with the eyes of your soul."

The sun flashed here and there in the water like the play of a smile.

"Are you seeing the face of the Great Spirit, my son?"

"Yes, Father."

"You can see the reflection of Wacunda's face in clear pools," said the chief, "but only when your mind

is still and your soul has seeing eyes. Be still, my son,
and know the Presence of the Great Spirit in this
place."

The head chief of the Otoe tribe and his youngest
son worshiped until sundown of that warm, quiet day.

Sharp Claws pointed to a bald eagle preparing to pounce upon its prey.

On their way back to the village Sharp Claws
pointed to a bald eagle preparing to pounce upon its
prey.

Chief Take-Blanket-Away shot the eagle, and he
and the boy plucked its long feathers to add to the
chief's many-feathered headdress which he wore on
special occasions.

"You may have some of these feathers to save for
your own headdress, my son," the chief said, with a
smile. "And when you are a grown man you will remember the day that we saw and killed this big eagle."

Soon came an eventful day, when the sacred game, Tow-wa, was played.

The sons of the head chief knew that this game was played in the Warm Moons, and then, only at such times when sad people needed cheering. They knew that every tepee in the village possessed a blue, yellow, purple, brown, or green ball stick and a soft ball of buffalo hide held in readiness for the playing of this game, for it was the most sacred, most important game of the Otoe tribe. And they knew, too, that among the treasures in their father's tepee was the sacred ball stick, the only ball stick allowed a coat of red paint. It was the "leading stick" and was used, always, to start the game.

They knew that among the treasures in their father's tepee was the sacred ball stick, the only ball stick allowed a coat of red paint.

The four brothers were too young to join in the playing of the game, but they ran with the other small boys of the village, following the players from goal to goal, a distance of about a mile and a half.

How lustily their song-filled throats joined in the singing of the ball-game song after a woman who had fasted first sang it from her tepee.

> *Ee wah hah-in-yah no no*
> *Ho wah coo-jah hah-in-yah no*
> *Ah-hee-skee-jah hon neah nah wee.*

Which means:

> We have it: the stick and the ball.
> We have it,
> We have it,
> Our ball that is played in honor of the sad.

When night came they were as tired as young boys can be, but, like true braves they gave no sign of it and were ready as ever for their Sleep Man tales.

"Tonight you shall hear again the origin of Tow-wa, the ball game," announced their father after they had settled quietly down upon their beds of buffalo hides.

"Good!" exclaimed Sunlight. "We want to hear how our tribe first came to play the game."

In the far-back times the older people were busy hunting, making arrowheads, weaving, and decorating their costumes and tepees, but the young people were often at a loss for something to do and often got into mischief.

The fact that her four sons were constantly getting into trouble of some kind worried a certain woman of the tribe, so she went into her tepee to fast and to study and to sing prayers to the Great Spirit.

She felt that Wacunda must direct her imagination to fashion something of interest for the young people; she must think of some kind of amusement for them.

After fasting four Suns and four Sleeps she came out of her tepee to face the rising sun. Then she sent her four sons out hunting.

"Each of you must bring me what you first shoot with your bows and arrows," she directed.

The eldest son brought her a deer. The next-to-eldest son brought her a wild turkey. The third son brought her a grouse, and the youngest son brought her a young buffalo.

"This is what I want," she announced, and then she took the hide of the buffalo, tanned it, and used the softest part to make a ball.

After that she gave directions to her sons for the making of ball sticks with which to play a game.

She fasted and studied and sang prayers to the Great Spirit yet another four Suns and four Sleeps, and on the last day of her fasting all the clans assembled in front of her tepee.

The woman came out of the tepee to face the rising sun. Then she gave out the rules for the playing of the game.

She pointed to a hill toward Boo-wah-lay, the Place of the Setting Sun, and to a tree toward Boo-wah-hoo, the Place of the Rising Sun, and said these were goals toward which each two groups were to play.

She announced that the Bear clan should play the Beaver clan first, followed by the other clans, one against another.

"You are to play four full games by striking the ball with your sticks until one side or the other makes a goal," she said. "The clan which first makes a goal is the winner."

Then she taught the people the song which should be sung at the beginning of each of the four games, after a woman who had fasted had first sung the song from her tepee:

Ee wah hah-in-yah no no
Ho wah coo-jah hah-in-yah no
Ah-hee-skee-jah hon neah nah wee.

After that the game began. The Bear and the Beaver clans took their places. The ball was handled by an old man who acted as referee. Each player touched the ball to insure himself against bad luck in the game, and after that all the sticks were put together for an instant before the players started to knock the ball.

The woman had given directions for a sacred tepee stick to be painted red. She said it must be the only one of its kind. It was to be the "leading stick" of the game, and used only by members of the Bear clan. When not in use it was to be kept in the tepee of the head chief and guarded, with the rest of the sacred possessions, by the Pipe Man.

That is why you see the red ball stick hanging here in our tepee today, along with the Pipe of Peace and my coup stick and the secret things in the medicine bag.

When Chief Take-Blanket-Away had finished his story, he sat puffing at his pipe for many breaths and staring into the shadows that lurked in the doorway. His trained ears caught the restless stirring of the hobbled horses grazing near the tepee. The sound was like wind under wild-rose bushes. Then he turned and regarded the serious faces of his sons.

"You shall play the game when you are older," he said, "and you must remember that a game is enjoyable only when braves play fairly and for the pleasure of playing. You must think, too, of the sick people and of those who are bereaved, for it is in their honor we play this game."

Chapter 6

THE BEAR CLAN ON A CAMPING TRIP

"WAKE UP, MY SONS!" came Circling Eagle's singing voice. "The silver moccasins of dawn are changing to beaded ones of wild-rose tint! Wake up, and let us start on our journey!"

The word "journey" brought the four boys to their feet at once. "Where are we going?" they all demanded to know.

"Some of the families of our clan are going to make camp along the far river at the foot of the sandhills," their mother informed them. "We shall fish and hunt there for maybe two moons, and before we return to the village we shall pick sandhill plums to bring home with us."

With war whoops the boys started to dance wildly about the wigwam, but their mother put a stop to their antics by commanding them to eat their breakfast and prepare to help her pack their travois with the rolled-up summer tepee, bundles of blankets, and par-

fleches of dried meat and corn which they would use
when there happened to be no fresh meat or vegetables
on hand.

Chief Take-Blanket-Away had already laid out his
fishing poles and lines, with his hooks of pointed and
barbed bone. Now he was giving the Pipe Man last-
minute instructions and an added warning about the
safeguarding of the Peace Pipe and the secret possessions in the lodge during the family's absence.

The chief of the Elk clan, being village manager
during the three Spring Moons, was coming to the
head chief for final council, and then the little band of
Bear clan families would be ready to start.

The sons of the head chief gulped down their
breakfast of pemmican cakes* and wild honey. They
cleaned their polished clay bowls and their horn spoons,
and then helped their mother pack them onto the
travois with the rest of the dishes and cooking utensils.

The last thing Circling Eagle put in was a willow
basket filled with her personal trinkets and her berry-
juice face paint, for she did not intend to neglect her
appearance merely because they were to be away on
a camping trip.

In the basket with her face paint were her necklace of wampum and her silver bracelets for which she
had traded with tribes from the far south, her beaded
headband, and her hawk's-wing fan. And she had put
in plenty of the lovely beads carved out of bone and
painted with dyes, tiny shells, and polished pebbles,
with which to decorate any new garment she might

---

* Pemmican cakes are made of meat, dried and pounded to a pulp.

make while away. Tiny holes had been carefully drilled in the ends of these beads so that she could string them easily.

When everything was packed, the boys helped their mother harness to a horse the upper ends of the two long poles of the travois; then they leaped upon the backs of their own spotted ponies and sat waiting for their father to lead the procession, riding on the back of his beautiful pinto.

At last they were on their way. The men rode ahead, occasionally using their quirts to make the ponies trot, while the squaws followed, each riding a horse drawing a travois. Their dogs leaped about them, barking excitedly.

Members of the other clans stood in the doors of

The squaws followed, each riding a horse drawing a travois.

their lodges to wave good-by, promising to see that everything progressed well in the village during their absence.

Over the trail to the far river at the foot of the sandhills went the colorful band on their two-and-a-half-day trek. Wind anemones sprinkled the trail, and the pink flower of the wild onion blushed coyly in the thick mats of buffalo grass along the way. Now and then a meadow lark would burst into song, perched on some tall spike of yucca bloom. And like a burst of song the wild-plum blossoms came into sight, as the Indians reached the sandhills near the river at noon of the third day.

There, in an open space above the river, the squaws pitched the buffalo-hide tepees. Soon a cook fire was burning out in front of each tepee, and on a forked stick on the side away from the smoke a long pole was propped, on the end of which dangled a hunk of fresh meat on a long cord.

When the meat began to cook, the women placed bowls beneath it to catch the drippings for gravy. A wedge-shaped wooden sail, fastened to the cord at an angle, caught the breeze and kept the meat turning. The fragrance of the meat filled the new camp and made the people very hungry.

They were hungry, and they were happy, out there by the golden-brown hills splotched with green, out under a blue and cloud-tumbled sky.

In the afternoon everyone went fishing along the wooded bank of the river.

Cottonwood trees towered above the water, and

the air was rich with the scent of cedar. A wild deer, drinking thirstily where the water bubbled over white pebbles, darted nimbly away into the cedar gloom. A woodpecker lightly beat his "signal drums" from a hollow tree.

Sharp Claws and Sunlight were hunting a new spot in which to try their fishing luck, when Sharp Claws discovered the shells of some river clams lying beside the stream.

"Look!" he cried. "Can we make some new fish-hooks out of these shells?"

"Yes, we can," Sunlight answered. "Father showed me how to carve the hooks out and to make them barbed. And he showed me how to drill tiny holes in the ends to fasten the fishing line through."

"I'll put the shells into my pouch and take them back to camp. This evening you'll teach me how to make the hooks, won't you?"

"Of course I will," his big brother told him, importantly, "and I'll show you how to make them out of bone, too."

At Sundown Sharp Claws and Sunlight came out of the small, wooded area onto a low, open space leading into a shallow spot thick with new, green cattails and watercress.

Out in the middle of the river the water was still deep, but here at the edge was an enticing wading pool for little Picture-in-the-Water, the spotted sandpiper, and the killdeer.

Suddenly the air was filled with a loud, shrill trilling. It sounded near, and then far.

"What is that strange sound?" cried Sharp Claws.
"I don't know what it is, and I can't locate it," replied Sunlight. "It seems to be right beside us, and then it seems to be over across the river somewhere."

"There! The sound is coming from the throats of those giant birds!" Sharp Claws shouted, pointing at three sandhill cranes alighting on the bank. "They are like little Picture-in-the-Water, but they are taller than you are, Sunlight! They are big Picture-in-the-Water, I guess."

"What high legs they have!" Sunlight answered. "Let's keep very quiet, and watch them."

The three tall birds looked cautiously around, then they trilled again, and almost immediately five or six other sandhill cranes arrived and began to fish in the water with their swordlike bills, while the first three cranes acted as sentinels for the flock.

"I wish I had a sword like they have! Maybe I would have better luck fishing!" whispered Sharp Claws.

"You'll have good luck tomorrow with the new hooks we are going to make out of those clam shells," Sunlight told him.

"Look!" the younger boy whispered excitedly. "Big Picture-in-the-Water has caught a frog. See him wriggle!"

"Another one has caught a lizard in his bill," Sunlight said, pointing at him. "Let us slip away without frightening these fellows. I believe we can cut across this meadow land and arrive at camp in a shorter time than we would if we were to follow the riverbank."

"Look! Big Picture-in-the-Water has caught a frog!"

The boys started to creep away, but the three sentinel cranes saw them and set up a warning cry.

Immediately the flock arose into the air, and,

stretching their necks at full length, they flapped their huge wings to carry them over to a group of near-by cottonwood trees.

Sharp Claws and Sunlight caught sight of large nests built into the tops of the tall trees, and as they looked a fledgling came tumbling out of one of the nests.

"Ho! Poor little papoose!" exclaimed Sunlight. "They'd better tie that fellow to a cradle board!"

Such a commotion as went up when the big birds saw the fledgling fall to the ground!

"The old birds are having a real powwow over him, aren't they?" Sharp Claws remarked. "And they're making him fly up, a little at a time, till he gets back to his lodge! That'll teach him to stay at home till they say he can go out!"

When they arrived at camp they found that all the others had been back for some time.

"Where did you go?" Surprise demanded to know. "We wanted you to see a nest we found. A nest of wild turkey's eggs——"

"Dirty-white eggs with reddish spots!" interposed Spotted Tail.

"Yes, and I nearly stepped on the eggs before I saw them!" finished Surprise.

Sharp Claws shouted his news: "*We* saw some giant birds that are taller than we are!"

"Aw, tell that to the Sleep Man!" scoffed Spotted Tail.

"No, really! Big Picture-in-the-Water, we called them! Their heads looked shaved—or bald, maybe—

and their eyes are the color of bittersweet berries,"
Sunlight told them.

"They have built their lodges in the tops of some
tall trees. There's a whole village of lodges!" he added

Chief Take-Blanket-Away had been sitting in front
of the tepee, polishing his arrow shafts by passing
them through holes drilled in a thin, flat rock. He
looked up, now, and smiled at his sons.

"Big Picture-in-the-Water is a good name for this
giant bird," he said. "Another name for him is 'Bird-
on-Stilts.' Shall I tell you how this big bird got that
name?"

"I knew there was a 'How' story about him!" Sharp
Claws shouted.

"After supper I will tell you the story," Chief Take-
Blanket-Away answered. "Just now I believe our
kettle of fish is ready to eat. Doesn't it smell good?"

Four noses began to sniff the air.

"Big Picture-in-the-Water was out fishing, too. I
hope he went back, after we left, and finished getting
his supper," Sunlight said.

"And I hope he will take a nice juicy lizard back
to the papoose that fell out of the nest!" added Sharp
Claws.

❦

In the far-back times, shortly after The First Four
Brothers Came out of the Waters, all the birds of the
earth looked exactly alike. They were all of one big
tribe and spoke the same tongue. They built their
lodges exactly alike, in one huge village of tall trees,
and they ate the same kind of food.

This village was near a shallow river. The birds enjoyed bathing and drinking in the river, and they liked to eat the weed seeds and tiny berries that grew along the edge of the river. They even liked to peep over the edge of the bank to gaze at their pictured faces in the water.

One day Wacunda told the bird tribe that he was going to send a big flood, soon, to widen the river.

He said, "You birds must stay away from the edge of this river so you won't get drowned. I have put a little pond in yonder meadow land for you to use, and you will like it just as well as the river."

But some of the birds didn't like to be told to stay away from the river. They thought they were wise enough to look after themselves, and so they ventured down there every day.

Then, without any more warning, the flood came. It descended so suddenly, and with such a roaring and slashing of waters, that the birds who had disobeyed Wacunda were caught in the midst of it and tossed about on the big waves like bits of foam. Their wings were heavy with water, and their legs were too short to reach bottom, even when the floodwaters receded, leaving only a very wide river. They were about to drown when one of the birds who had obeyed Wacunda prayed, "O Wacunda, those birds were very foolish children, and I know they are sorry they disobeyed You. Will You not put some stilts on my short legs so that I can wade into the river and rescue them?"

Wacunda smiled down upon the water, and it began to sparkle with light. He sent a gentle breeze to float the naughty birds toward the more shallow water near the edge of the river. Then He said to the bird who had prayed to Him, "Look at yourself. You have stilts with which to wade into the water—deeper water than you have ever tried. Go now and rescue my disobedient children."

The bird looked down at his legs and saw that he was, indeed, on stilts, for the ground looked much farther away. He looked at his brother birds and saw that they, too, were on stilts. And he noticed that they were all much larger birds than they had been before.

These birds of a new clan drew themselves up proudly, and began to trill in a loud chorus, to let the frightened birds on the water know that help was coming. Then, without another wasted moment they waded into the water, caught the wings of their drowning brothers in their long beaks, and carried them to shore.

Ever since that day there have been many different clans of birds. Some with tall legs, many with short legs; and all clans were given different-colored feathers and different songs.

The sandhill crane is known as the Bird-on-Stilts because of the tall legs Wacunda gave him on that occasion. And he has been, to this day, a bird of great courage and wisdom.

"*Yah-wah shee-geh!*" Circling Eagle called from inside the tepee.

"Aw! Did that old Sleep Man tag us away down here?" Spotted Tail snorted indignantly.

"The trail of the Evening Star leads everywhere," answered his mother. "And the moccasins of Po-too Yeo never fail to find it."

So, without further argument, the boys went to bed.

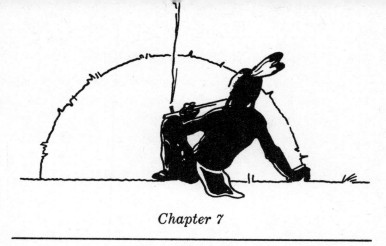

Chapter 7

A VISITOR

THE TWO MOONS spent at the foot of the sandhills were full of pleasure and adventure for the children of the Bear clan families.

They saw birds and animals that were entirely new to them, and were told, at bedtime, the legends of how these creatures came to be in the world. In fact, *most* of their knowledge had been gained through the telling of legends.

On very warm days the Indians would bathe or swim in the river, drying themselves in the sun. And sometimes they would wander in the spotted shade of the woods along the riverbanks, picking wild strawberries in their season, and later the wild raspberries.

Just before leaving for home the sandhill plums were ripe, and the women and children picked many basketfuls to take back with them. As well as for themselves they picked enough to take to the clans who had remained in the village.

Since it was Chief Take-Blanket-Away's responsibility to be back in the village at the beginning of the Summer Moons, he gave instructions, one day, to pack up for the return journey. And so the two-and-a-half-day trek back to the Otoe village began.

Now, it was in the Moon-of-the-wild-blackberries. Sunlight, Spotted Tail, Surprise, and Sharp Claws were out picking berries for the evening meal when they saw a stranger, an old man, gliding on noiseless moccasined feet along the trail which lay, like a buck-

They saw a stranger gliding along the trail.

skin whip lash, at the foot of the knoll where they stood. The path led to the Otoe village.

"I wonder what tribe that man is from," said Spotted Tail in an anxious whisper, his heart beating like a tomtom.

"I wonder why he is here!" Sunlight's heart, too, beat like a tomtom.

"Let's go and see," suggested Sharp Claws, and so they hurriedly filled their baskets and ran back to their lodge.

They found Circling Eagle cooking supper on a fire outside the tepee.

Their guest was Coming Daylight, a friendly visitor from the Kaw tribe encamped many, many steps away.

They all sat down on the ground, and then Circling Eagle served bowls of steaming greens, little corn-cakes fried in oil from sunflower seeds, roasted prairie hen, and some of the fresh blackberries which the boys had brought home.

Coming Daylight ate heartily, for his long journey had given him an appetite.

When the meal was over Chief Take-Blanket-Away and his guest sat in the friendly dusk, smoking their pipes together.

Take-Blanket-Away blew his smoke to Todja-dowa, the four winds, then to the sky, then to the earth; and then Coming Daylight blew his smoke to the four winds, then to the sky, then to the earth.

After that they visited, partly by sign language, and partly with words of both tongues, for each of the men understood some of the other's language.

The four boys edged close and listened, fascinated, to stories of bravery and adventure, and to songs which Coming Daylight sang for his host.

The old man's last song was a hunting song which

he had composed himself; and by singing it he bestowed an honor upon his host, for although every red man had a song of his own, he did not sing it for just anyone. This hunting song was a story of his own life. He sang:

> I lived in a sturdy wigwam
> Out on the windy plains.
> And when I grew to manhood
> My father said to me:
> "Here is your bow and arrow,
> Go kill 'em—bring 'em home!"
> And so I became a hunter,
> A hunter strong and wise.
> Today I'm old and weary
> And I'm longing for the chase—
> Longing for the buffalo, the elk, the antelope.
> But soon I will be leaving this world,
> And then I'll be
> Using my bow and arrow
> In my Happy-Hunting-Ground.*

His tones rose and fell in weird cadences, and his body swayed as from a strong wind blowing.

---

* Composed and owned by Coming Daylight of the Kaw tribe now at Washunga, Oklahoma.

When he had finished, his leatherlike face masked the look of stars above low clouds, and resumed its stolid expression. He said in an even tone:
"Now I am going to tell these young braves a story before they go to bed."

"Good," chorused the boys all in one breath, for they understood the Kaw visitor enough to enjoy a story, and so they came and sat at his feet.

"I shall tell you how Too-loo-lah, the rainbow, got its colors. This is one of the stories Kaw tribesmen tell around their lodge fires."

The delicate flowers of the Spring Moons bloom, and then they die. Gorgeous blossoms of Summer Moons live a little longer and they, too, die. The riotous shades of autumn flowers flourish and then they are no more. We think they are gone forever—but, no! When the rainbow (the Too-loo-lah in our tongue) appears after a shower we see them again, these beautiful flowers of many colors, in the sky. The rainbow is the flowers' Land of the Hereafter.

"That is a beautiful story about beautiful things," said Sharp Claws. "Will you tell us *another* 'How' story?"

"Shall I tell you what the people of my tribe call the tall flower* that grows upon the prairie, and how it got its name?"

"Please!" begged Sharp Claws.

"It always comes just at the time of the green

---
* Indigo flower.

corn," said Coming Daylight, "to tell us of the approach of the Warm Season."

⇔

One time an old man stood at the edge of a small cornfield and looked at this flower which was growing near by.

Suddenly a voice came from the flower, saying, "Why-nee-yah," which means in our tongue, "Indian, go!"

"Why-nee-yah," it repeated. "This is the beginning of the Warm Season, and you will soon have roasting ears for your feasts. Go and cultivate that you may have much corn!"

The old man almost forgot to do as the flower instructed him, although he finally remembered; and that is why the flower returns every year to remind the people to cultivate their corn and not to stand idle.

⇔

"*Yah-wah shee-geh!*" called Circling Eagle in the voice that was soft-toned like the village announcer's bell. "The Sleep Man will find you out in the dark if you do not come in at once!"

And so, after thanking their visitor for entertaining them, the boys reluctantly went into the tepee.

They settled down upon their beds and lay gazing out through the open door of the lodge at the moonshod prairie where the wind breathed softly in the gulleys and a brown thrasher quavered a night song from a far-off cottonwood tree.

While they lay there Circling Eagle sang to them a little song they loved, about the stars:

One by one
The stars are lighted by the sun
Before he retires to his lodge for rest.
It is his last duty of the day.

Over and over she sang the song, until the Sleep
Man had made his noiseless visit to the darkened tepee.

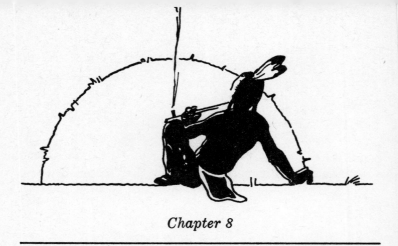

Chapter 8

HOW CON-THA GAH, THE COYOTE, GOT THE NAME OF BEING A THIEF

"DOE-CHEE-ING-GAH, the meadow lark, sits near by and sings," Coming Daylight remarked the next morning as the boys greeted him outside the tepee.

"Is that a sign of something?" Sunlight inquired.

"It is the sign of the coming of a visitor from another tribe," was Coming Daylight's answer.

"Perhaps you are that visitor," suggested Sharp Claws.

"But I am already here," the old man returned, with a smile. "This visitor of whom Doe-chee-ing-gah sings is yet to come."

The little stream near the village was painted with sunrise when Coming Daylight started on his way to visit other tribes. Turning, as he left, he raised his hand in a benediction:

"May the Great Spirit bring sunrise to your hearts!" he said in solemn tones.

The visitor came that evening, as the plains were being hooded with dusk. It was a runner from the Pawnee tribe announcing their head chief's desire to pay a visit to the Otoes, accompanied by all of his people.

His way of making his desires known was to have his runner offer the Otoe head chief little beaded sacks of fine tobacco. If the sacks were accepted the runner would know that his tribe was invited to come and camp for as long as four Suns and four Sleeps near the Otoe tribe's village at a given time of the moon.

Bear Chief Take-Blanket-Away accepted the beaded sacks and named the time of the full moon for the Pawnee tribe's visit. Then he sent word to the village announcer to go about the village ringing his deep-toned bell and spreading the news.

"Will there be a big feast, Father?" Sunlight wanted to know, after the Pawnee runner's moccasined feet had glided out of sight along the shadowed trail.

"Yes, my son, and much dancing and much giving of presents."

"I like to have visitors, for they always teach us new games and new stories!" Surprise said, as he entered the tepee carrying an armload of firewood.

"And you must learn well the games and stories— and the songs and dances, my sons," put in their mother, "so that you may teach them to *your* sons someday along with the legends of your own tribe."

"The Sleep Man is following the trail of the Evening Star," said Chief Take-Blanket Away. "What shall the story be tonight?"

"About how Con-tha gah, Swift Runner, the Coyote, got the name of being a thief," cried Sharp Claws
promptly.

"Does this story belong to the Otoe tribe, Father?"
asked Sunlight.

"It has been told around our lodge fires so many,
many generations that no one knows from where it
came. At least it belongs to the Otoes now," the father
replied. "Well," he began——

It was late in the season when the leaves put on
their warpaint; when we hear the war drums of the
wind.

An old man, living quite alone on the prairie, had
been storing food in his wigwam in preparation for
the Snow Season.

"It will come early; I know the signs!" he spoke
aloud, and only Ma-coe-gee, the screech owl, made re-
ply. "Did I not see the geese fly toward the ever-warm
country more than fourteen Suns ago? The muskrat
has built his house earlier than usual; the fish have
run up-creek to spawn, instead of waiting; the frog
has buried himself two feet in mud; all the animals
have thicker fur——"

"What is that you say about the animals' fur,
Grandpa?" This was the yipping voice of Swift Runner, the Coyote. The tall, thin old man peered out into
the growing dusk.

"I have not eyes to see in the dark like yours, friend
Swift Runner, but my ears know your voice. Come in
and have supper with me. I am a lonely old man."

Con-tha gah's eyes were yellow in the light of the
lodge fire. His stomach was snarling with hunger, and
his tongue dripped water at the sight of the bowl of
steaming parched corn. He decided to play a trick on
the old man so that he might have all of the supper
instead of only half of it. It did not matter to him
that the old man's legs and arms were as thin as willow
sticks and that his stomach appeared to be rubbing
his backbone. Con-tha gah was looking out only for
himself.

"Grandpa," he said, "the trees of all tribes are
having a big powwow tonight, and I was sent to invite
you."

When he spoke, the old man's voice broke because
he was made so happy. He hurried to the far side of
the wigwam and put on his feathered headdress. He
painted his face. He put on his beaded vest and his
beaded loincloth. Then, in his beaded moccasins he
ran out to dance with the trees. He had forgotten to
eat his supper. And the coyote did not remind him.
A grin broke out all over his face after the old man
had gone. He ate all of the steaming parched corn,
and everything the poor old man had in store.

After he had eaten the last bite to be found, the
coyote sneaked out and ran on wind footsteps across
the prairie where he stood upon a knoll and howled at
the rising moon whose blazing eye accused him of being
a thief.

The old man went to the place along the river to
which Swift Runner had directed him. There he saw
all the tribes of trees swaying in the wind while they

He stood upon a knoll and howled at the moon.

sang—now high, now low—to the tomtom of the wind.

"Hoh!" the old man cried. "The dance has begun. I can see the bending of the trees and I can hear their leaves singing as they fall!"

He was so full of joy that he, too, began to dance. The harder the wind blew, the harder he danced.

His spiderlike legs and arms were fantastic against the sky. At times his big right fist appeared to be juggling the rising moon, while in his left hand he shook a feathered rattle.

As the moon rose higher he resembled a spider sus-

His spiderlike legs and arms were fantastic against the sky. At times his big right fist appeared to be juggling the rising moon, while in his left hand he shook a feathered rattle.

pended on a cobweb from the sky. That is what the coyote thought, as he caught sight of him, on his way back to his hole in the side of the hill.

All night and all the next day he danced and sang with the trees, until the wind quit blowing. Then he fell exhausted to the ground.

While he lay there, resting, he looked up into the branches, and began talking to the trees:

"Friends," he said, "I had forgotten how well I liked to dance, for I am growing old. It was good of you to invite me here, and now I will go to my wigwam and bring back food for a feast."

He hurried home, but found no food left in his storehouse. The coyote was nowhere in sight! And from that day to this he is known as Mah-nee cath-ee, the thief.

"Now, boys, go to sleep," put in Circling Eagle, "for we must arise when the east is pale, to begin preparations for the coming of our guests at the time of the full moon. Your father has many suns of planning ahead of him, and I, as well as the other women, must set about making beaded gifts for the visitors."

And so the boys fell asleep, listening to the dusk lullaby of the mother Prairie out there in the breathless starlight.

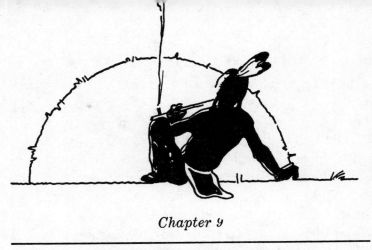

Chapter 9

TRIBAL CELEBRATIONS

THE TIME OF THE FULL MOON had come. Excitement stirred among the Otoe people, for their Pawnee visitors had begun to arrive and were setting up their portable summer tepees in a camp of their own just outside the village of the Otoes.

The tepee of the Pawnee head chief had already been erected in the center of the huge circle marked off by the Otoes, and each tepee now being set up had its doorway facing the sunrise sky.

Upon his arrival the Pawnee head chief had approached the Otoe village, giving the peace sign. He was greeted by Chief Take-Blanket-Away.

At dusk Sunlight, Spotted Tail, Surprise, and Sharp Claws wandered over to the Pawnee camp and tried, in a shy way, to make friends with two or three of the boys of the visiting tribe.

As they passed one of the tepees they saw a Pawnee mother rocking her papoose to sleep.

The Pawnee chief approached the Otoe village, giving the peace sign in greeting.

He was a round little fellow with ebony eyes that looked as if they would never go shut! He lay on his cradle board and blinked at the dazzling moon.

Painted above his head, on this cottonwood cradle board, was a rainbow, "the arch above the earth"; for Pawnee mothers and fathers believe that if they decorate the cradle boards in this manner their papooses will be watched over by the Powers of the West.

As she sang to the papoose the mother bounced him gently up and down during the first three phrases of the song and swayed him from side to side during the remainder of it.

Hao-u-wa-ri. . . Ha-u-o
Hao-u-wa-ri. . . Ha-u-o
Ha-u-o.

The Otoe boys heard these words in a tongue which was unfamiliar to them, but they liked the sound of it.

Hao-u-wa-ri. . . Ha-u-o
Hao-u-wa-ri. . . Ha-u-o
Ha-u-o.

sang the mother over and over in a droning voice that made the boys think of bees in a patch of wild clover. On and on it droned until the ebony eyes became hazy with dreams, and the eyelids fluttered shut like the wings of little birds.

"The Sleep Man has got him at last," laughed Sunlight, as they moved on.

"See that tepee with the otter painted on it!" Spotted Tail exclaimed. "It has marks of bear claws on it, too."

"Yes," spoke a voice in their own tongue, "the otter is the supreme beast, and the wisest; and the bear, to us, is a symbol of the sun."

Standing behind them was a Pawnee boy not much taller than Sunlight.

"You wonder how I happen to speak your tongue," the boy chuckled, as the Otoe boys stared at him. "My grandmother is from the Otoe tribe, and she taught me, you see."

"Then you can tell us many things about your tribal customs; and tonight, when the powwow begins, you can tell us the meaning of all the songs and dances given by your people!" suggested Sunlight.

"I will gladly do that," assented the Pawnee boy, "and now tell me your names so that we can really be friends. My name is Swift Moccasin."

"My name is Ma-schaay, Sunlight," replied the eldest of the four brothers; "and this is Theen-jaay-klay-ea, Spotted Tail; Washungalay, Surprise; and Sayga-pahee, Sharp Claws." He pointed to each of his brothers as he named him.

After that the five boys wandered about together. Suddenly a tall chief strode in giant strides through the encampment. He called his people in a loud, commanding voice. Following was a group of braves who stopped in the middle of the new-made village and began to beat upon a big drum and to sing in high-pitched eerie voices.

The boys knew they were announcing that they were ready to start the festivities, and their hearts pounded like small tomtoms in their throats.

The Otoe people came over at once, some in family groups, some in groups of old men, and children; and a few strolled over alone. They sat upon the ground, or stood about, ready to be entertained by their guests.

The Pawnee dancers formed an immense circle inside of which sat the six or seven drummers around a huge drum. As the drummers beat a continuous "tom-tom-tom-tom" lusty throats shouted and wailed the songs which belonged to each dance. The sound was a strange mixture of a wailing coyote chorus and the minor music of a storm-brewing wind.

First came the Buffalo Dance, wherein a brave in the center flung a string of buffalo hoofs to a Pawnee maiden wearing on her head a pair of buffalo horns, as did all the other women in the circle.

As she held the hoofs she danced beside the young man until she chose to fling the hoofs to another brave who then came and danced beside her, while the first brave retired to the circle.

Both dancers imitated buffaloes—bellowing, pawing the earth, flinging up dust and catching it on their backs, and moving their heads from side to side.

This caused the Otoe boys to laugh. They decided to try that dance themselves sometime.

Next came the Wolf Dance, which was given by the men alone. "Pawnee means 'wolf,'" Swift Moccasin explained to the Otoe boys. "This is our tribal dance."

Then followed other dances, some of them very stiff and solemn, some full of antics which made everyone laugh.

Preceding the last dance, which was called "The Pipe Dance of the Corn Festival," the Otoe head chief presented to the Pawnee head chief a robe of woven fur strips, carved deer-hoof knee rattles, a willow basket, and a spotted pony.

The gifts were received with song and beating of drums.

For the Pipe Dance the men were naked, except for a black breechcloth, and they were wrapped in blankets of midnight black.

The dancers started from the north side of the circle; the head chief was in the lead, and on each side of him a singer and a drummer walked. The proces-

sion of men sang and danced all the way around the
circle to the west side, where they stopped and faced
the east. The Pawnee chief then set an ear of white
corn on a mound of dirt, and then all the dancers sang
over and over:

PIPE DANCE

*Huh' A - ti - ra Moth - er Corn stands there. Moth-er stands there...

Moth - er stands there. .

*Author's Note: The Huh' represents an expulsion of breath. Breath of life for the
corn. This song was sung to me by a Pawnee girl.

"Why is half of that ear of corn painted blue?"
Sharp Claws inquired of their new friend.

"The blue is to represent the sky, and the white
represents the earth," Swift Moccasin explained.
"This dance is only *part* of a long corn festival. I think
it is splendid, don't you?"

"Oh, yes!" the boys assented in unison.

By this time the moon had ridden high on its path-
way across the sky. A shooting star blinded the night.
Spotted Tail pointed toward the streak of light.
"It is a blazing arrow of the fire gods!" he whispered.

At that moment the Otoe boys saw their mother
coming in search of them. "*Yah-wah shee-geh*," she
said in a low voice, when she had found them.

And so the boys bade the Pawnee boy a reluctant
good night.

"That was a fine spotted pony you gave the Pawnee

---

* Corn is called "mother" because of its nourishing milk.

A shooting star blinded the night.

chief tonight, Father," said Sunlight, when they were all lying on their beds.

"Yes, my son," replied Chief Take-Blanket-Away. "All of our horses are splendid."

"Father, how did the horse happen to become the friend of the red man?" asked Sharp Claws. "They were all running wild on these plains and hills at one time, weren't they?"

"Another 'How' Story?" asked their father. "Well, then——"

In the far-back times all the wild beasts of the forest and prairie held a council to decide which of their company should comply with Man's request and become his friend.

They sat about the council fire with folded arms and clamped lips and looked at the man with the cold of Winter Moons in their eyes. Not one of the animals wanted to give up his freedom.

At last the man turned away and started with heavy feet and heavier heart down the trail.

When he had gone but a few steps Shoo-nea, the little wild horse, circled the council fire and neighed loudly. Then he followed the man and called, "Master, wait for me. I have decided to become your friend."

"It is good," replied the man, and in his voice was the song of the wind chimes.

The horse continued, "I will work for you, lead you out of danger, go on the warpath with you, and obey your every command. I have spoken."

"That is good," the man repeated, and he patted the neck of the little horse.

"Some of my brother horses are still wild," said Shoo-nea, "but you will be able to tame them because of my regard for you."

A faint sound came to the quick ears of the man. Swiftly he put his ear to the ground. "I hear the soft pad-padding of feet," he told the horse. "It is the sound of a smaller animal than you."

"It is Shoo-kan nea, the dog," said Shoo-nea.

When the dog reached the man and the horse he was all out of breath and his tongue lolled out of the corner of his mouth.

"The horse is my best friend," he panted at last, "and where he goes I go. Take me, Master, and I will be your friend too! I have spoken."

"It is good," said the man again. "Come with us, Shoo-kan nea."

"I will watch over you at night," the dog promised

as he trotted along. "I will go hunting with you during the day."

"The horse and dog have been man's friend ever since that time," Chief Take-Blanket-Away said in conclusion.

"Now I can see the shadow of the Sleep Man on the tepee wall," Circling Eagle spoke warningly. "We must all get plenty of sleep so that tomorrow our eyes may hold the sunlight and our hearts may be full of song."

"Yes," agreed the chief, "and you boys may go with me to select the pony for tomorrow evening's giving."

And so, with this thrilling promise tucked away in their minds, the boys dropped off to sleep.

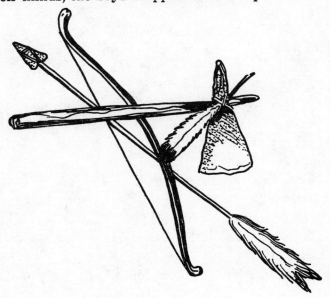

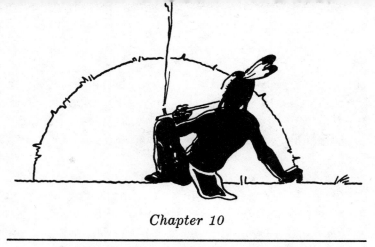

Chapter 10

THE STORY OF THE PEACE PIPE

AFTER the Pawnee visitors had returned to their own
village the Otoe tribe settled down to the everyday
habits of living once more. The women worked at their
basketry and beading. They made dyes from berry
juices and roots with which to paint designs upon their
dresses and fancywork while the men sharpened their
arrowheads and their hunting knives, and spent hours
at painting new symbols upon their summer tepees.

All members of the tribe studied the stars every
night in search of signs to guide them in their hunting,
in their celebration, and in their love making.

This evening, as Chief Take-Blanket-Away sat
alone in the starlight in front of his lodge, he was
searching for a sign in the heavens which would tell
him of coming rain; for, all through the Summer
Moons the red men of the plains had not heard the
whirring of the Thunder Bird's wings nor the tiptoeing of rain upon their corn. The cruel sun had scorched

the prairie grasses and had baked the soil in its oven heat. The little stream near the village was whispering hoarsely out of a dry throat; whispering warningly of tragedies which having no water can bring to a village.

As the chief sat there feeling the hot silence of the night he heard the pleading notes of a flageolet and knew that somewhere in the village a brave was letting a maiden know that he loved her. The chief knew that the happiness of his people rested upon his ability to arouse the sympathy of the Rain Gods; and so he resolved to begin, at dawn, a ritual to bring the parching drouth to an end.

The next morning, when the sun arose from his lodge and painted himself, the chief stepped outside his own lodge. The village was still quiet except for the barking of dogs. Lifting the flap of the tepee again, he called to the Pipe Man to bring out the Pipe of Peace from among the sacred possessions which he guarded day and night. The Pipe Man brought it, very soberly.

Chief Take-Blanket-Away took the Peace Pipe in his left hand. He threw back his head and drew in a deep breath of morning air. Then he walked slowly around his tepee.

Four times he walked around the tepee, and as he walked he sang:

> *O Wacunda,
> Let us have water from Thine hands to our hands!

---

* These songs are literal translations from the rain cycle of the Otoe tribe.—Used by permission of the head chief.

Send the raindrops for my children!
Send us water that our plants may drink!
O give me Thy power, Thou Great Spirit above!

At first the villagers heard the song of their head
chief as a stirring of their dreams; then, as he sang on
and on, they awoke to the knowledge of what he was
doing, and so they remained prayerfully in their
lodges.

Searing a path on the sky, the sun mounted higher
and higher. The chief looked searchingly for signs of
clouds, but not a fleck was in that wide tent of blue.

"The rain will come," he said to the Pipe Man, and
stood there, praying to the Great Spirit.

By the time the sun was noon high a change had
come into the air. Swallows flew so low they fanned
the dust with their wings. A smile came to the jet
eyes of Chief Take-Blanket-Away. He opened his lips
and sang to the swallows:

Why are you birds flying so low?
This is a sign of rain!
Always fly low, little swallows,
So that my people may know
When a change is coming!

He noticed dark clouds coming on the wings of the
wind; and then the joy in his voice carried to every
tepee in the village:

Yonder the dark clouds come!
It will rain, my people!
Listen to the sounds of it:
To Cogah, the muttering thunder;
To the precious drops as they come!
Listen to the noise—the great roaring.
Wah-wah!

Swallows flew so low they fanned the dust with their wings.

As the glistening drops began to fall the chief still stood outside his tepee singing his thanksgiving songs. To the raindrops he sang:

> You fill our hearts with happiness!
> O make our fields moist; be in our grain!
> All we need is help from you,
> O rolling clouds,
> O dripping rain!

To the lightning he sang:

> Yonder you flame!
> I do not fear your fire, Loo-glee,
> For you are a help to the red man.
> After the light I will recognize you as the rain
> And will give you a welcome!

All day it rained, and when Sunlight, Spotted Tail, Surprise, and Sharp Claws lay on their beds awaiting the telling of their evening story, the steady march of raindrops could be heard upon the steep sides of the tepee.

"Tonight, my sons," their father began, "I shall tell you the story of the Pipe of Peace."

"It is well." Circling Eagle looked up from the buckskin moccasin she was beading. "It is well, indeed, for our sons to know the story of our precious Secret to Happiness, our Good Heart Maker."

When the First Four Brothers Came out of the Waters, on the first morning of our world, they stretched themselves and said, "Let us set out to discover the secret to happiness, so that we can have it to pass on to our coming generations."

They named themselves the Bear clan. That is why the Bear clan is the head clan of our seven clans today.

They searched for many moons, and many moons; but since they did not know exactly what they were looking for they did not find their Secret to Happiness at once.

"We must make a symbol," Hana, the eldest, said. And so Higinee, the youngest, prayed to Wacunda:

> O Wacunda,
> Give me Thy thoughts!

Wacunda led the four brothers to a red clay hill and left them there.

Finally Higinee had a vision of a red clay pipe bowl, and he knew that this thought was Wacunda's.

The brothers molded a pipe bowl out of the red clay and recognized it as the Secret to Happiness about which they had dreamed.

Soon they met a man resembling a beaver (who later became head of the Beaver clan). The beaver offered to cut down a tree so that they might have a limb to whittle down for a mate to their red clay bowl (meaning a stem). The beaver gnawed at the tree until finally it came tumbling down at the Bear chief's feet. And so they whittled out a stem for the pipe.

"The pipe needs decoration," they all decided.

"Let us speak to Wacunda again," said Higinee.

After he had spoken again to the Great Spirit a voice came from behind a low cloud in the heavens: "I am the redheaded woodpecker," it announced as it swooped to earth. "The Master of the Upper Skies

"I am the bald eagle. Use me! Oh, use me!"

has sent me for you to use for decoration of your Secret
to Happiness. Take me, oh, take me!"
And so the brothers killed the woodpecker and used

its scarlet head on the stem of the pipe, about two inches from the mouthpiece.

Then came another voice from the sky: "I am the gray eagle," it announced. "You may have my feathers for decoration of your pipe. Use me, oh, use me!"

And so the brothers took two of the gray eagle's feathers and placed them at the head of the pipestem.

Then came another voice from the sky: "I am the bald eagle," it cried. "Use me, oh, use me!"

And so the brothers took two of the bald eagle's feathers and placed them behind those of the gray eagle.

Just then the queen eagle and the black eagle swooped down from the heavens, imploring the brothers to use their feathers also.

After two of the queen eagle's feathers had been placed on the pipe the black eagle offered two of his feathers, saying, "May your children step to the fourth hill (meaning the fourth generation). May they have tepees and lodge fires; may they use this Secret to Happiness, this Pipe of Peace, to settle all their troubles and to bring every good to their tribe. It shall be your Good Heart Maker. I have spoken."

And so the Pipe of Peace has been our Secret to Happiness, our Good Heart Maker, to this day. You have seen how it helped bring this welcome rain to our thirsty world, and you have seen how it helps us when we go hunting and when we go on the warpath. Good braves will guard this Secret to Happiness with their lives.

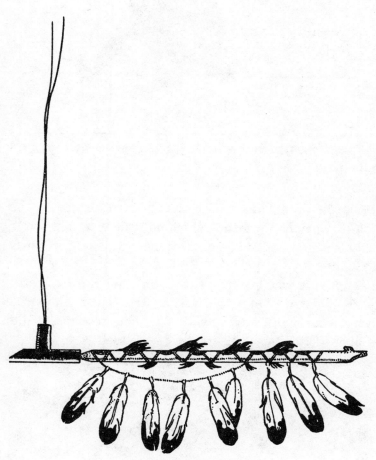

The Peace Pipe of the Otoe
(From a pencil drawing by Sharp Claws)

Chapter 11

HOW THE SEVEN CLANS CAME TOGETHER

THE CHILDREN of the tribe had played all day in the rain. They had waded in the mud; they had had water fights; they had made tiny canoes to paddle in pools of water.

Now it was evening again, and the rain was still sifting down—not so hard as at first, but with gentle insistence, as if, having waited so long to come, it did not want to stop until it had spent itself.

The rain was still sifting down.

Having played everything they could think of, the children were quite ready to sit quietly in their lodges and listen to the Sleep Man tales of the evening. And more than likely most of the tales of that evening were legends suggested by the falling rain.

The one Chief Take-Blanket-Away was about to tell his sons was a continuation of the one he had told on the previous night, when his singing of the Rain Cycle had suggested the story of the Peace Pipe.

He began before he seated himself.

When the First Four Brothers Came out of the Waters, on the first morning of our world, and named themselves the Bear clan, they roamed from place to place trying to discover the Secret to Happiness.

I have told you how these Brothers, Hana, Huhanguia, Higi, and Higinee, finally made a symbol—the Peace Pipe—which they smoked to help settle all their difficulties, and that they called this pipe their Secret to Happiness, their Good Heart Maker.

I have told you that they met a Beaver who cut down a tree so that the Bear clan might have a stem for the Peace Pipe, but I have not told you how the Bear met the Beaver.

Sharp Claws looked up, eagerly. "Do tell us, Father!" he begged.

Chief Take-Blanket-Away's eyes crinkled in the way his sons loved. He walked over to the bag of Secret Possessions which the Pipe Man always guarded, and taking out the Pipe of Peace he stroked the

large feathers of the gray eagle, the bald eagle, the queen eagle, and the black eagle. He touched, reverently, the little, carved woodpecker's head near the mouthpiece of the pipe.

"It was the making of this Good Heart Maker which brought our seven clans together," he said, as he came back to the pile of robes where the boys sat waiting. He seated himself, thoughtfully, with the Peace Pipe in his hands.

☕

The four members of the Bear clan thought they were the only people in the world, and so they claimed the earth as their own. But one time Higinee went away, alone, to seek a better place in which to work out their plans.

He had been walking over nappy blankets of green buffalo grass which stretched over low hills and crooked gullies. He had crossed zigzag streams where sycamore trees danced the Ghost Dance by moonlight, while watching willows shivered in cedar gloom.

Four times he had watched the dawn creep into the east on coral-moccasined feet, and four times he had seen the far western rim of the prairie drenched with sunset dyes. He had been gone four Suns and four Sleeps from where he had left his brothers.

Suddenly Higinee saw a man who looked not only like a man but also like a beaver. He was startled, for, as I said, he did not know there were any other persons except himself and his brothers.

"What are you doing in my world?" he demanded of the beaver.

The man who resembled a beaver was as surprised as he.

"What are *you* doing in *my* world?" he retorted.

"The world is mine!" Higinee shouted. "I am a member of the Bear clan. I could overpower you in one moment!" His voice rose to a growl, and the other man backed away.

"I am the chief of the Beaver clan," he said, as he continued to back away. "I thought that the world was mine, but if you say it is yours you may be right. My people and I have been here but a short time."

Just then Hana, Huhanguia, and Higi, who had been secretly following Higinee, came running up.

"Do not harm him, Higinee," cried Hana. "He may be our brother."

"Yes," the Beaver spoke up eagerly, "I *am* your brother. Let me and my people join you, and we will all go together to seek happiness for our children!"

And so the four brothers of the Bear clan accepted the Beaver as their brother.

"Let us give our new brother a name," Higi suggested.

"I shall call him Moon-jah nea, Little Bear," Hana, the head chief, announced.

"Then I shall call you Lah-wah nea, Little Beaver," retorted the Beaver.

They all laughed heartily at the joke, and then the Bear clan and the Beaver clan went along together, searching for more wisdom and complete happiness.

It was at that time that the Beaver offered to provide a stem for the bowl of the Peace Pipe.

And you remember how the woodpecker gave his head and the four eagles gave some of their feathers for the pipe's decoration?

After the Bear clan and the Beaver clan had traveled together for many Suns and many Suns, Hana, who had been guarding the Peace Pipe constantly, announced that they should find some way to make use of their Secret to Happiness.

"We need something to help settle our arguments," Higinee suggested.

They came to a sun-dappled river, one day, as the two clans were journeying along. As they paused to drink of the clear running water the Bear saw a man who resembled an elk lying asleep on the bank.

The Bear sprang at the elk and was about to kill him, when the elk cried out, "Please do not harm me! I should like to be your brother!"

But the brothers of the Bear clan said they would be ashamed of the elk's horns, and decided to kill him when the Beaver intervened.

"Why not let him live?" he suggested. "I believe he would make a good brother."

The elk took heart. "Yes, please let me live!" he begged. "I have, in my hoofs, something which will be very useful to you: it is *pageji*, the fire to set alight your Good Heart Maker. Have you not been praying for some way in which to *use* this pipe? Here it is. I have it!"

The brothers of the Bear clan looked at each other,

then they said to the elk, "We will accept you as our brother. Show us what you can do."

"I thank you," said the elk. "Now you can have cooked food to eat, and a fire to keep you warm when Todja-Omayda, the north wind, blows."

"That will be good!" the others agreed.

"Then I give you the light for your Secret to Happiness, your Good Heart Maker," said the elk.

He took some bark from a red willow, mashed it to pulp, and crammed it into the bowl of the pipe. Then, with friction from his hoofs, he made the first fire to light the Pipe of Peace.

"I shall call you Moon-jah, Big Bear," said Hana to the man who resembled an elk.

"Then I shall call you Tay-hah, Big Horn," retorted the elk, and the joke has been carried on from that day to this.

After the Bear clan, the Beaver clan, and the Elk clan had traveled together for many Suns and many Suns, they suddenly came upon someone who lay asleep on a sunny hilltop. It was a man who resembled a coyote.

The Bear captured the coyote, and then he said, "Come and be our brother."

The coyote was glad to bring his clan into the tribe, and so the four clans traveled along together.

"I shall call you Sayga nea, Little Claw," announced Hana.

"Then I shall call you Con-tha gah, Swift Runner," the coyote retorted. But he was interrupted by a terrifying scream from the heavens, and the strange

voice of a man who resembled an eagle called down
to them, "What are you people doing in my world?"
"But the world is ours!" the four clans exclaimed.
"No! It is mine! The Great Spirit made this earth
for me, only! Go back to the Waters from whence you
came!"

The Bear chief shouted back, "You are mistaken,
O Eagle chief, for I am the one who first set foot upon
Mother Earth, and so the earth is mine. But it is big
enough for us all. Why not come and be our brother?"

The kind answer made the eagle ashamed, and he
replied in a low voice, "I will come."

And so the eagle brought his clan of people; and
when all five clans had traveled along together for
many Suns and many Suns, they came upon a man
who resembled a snake.

"Do not harm me!" begged Too-neah Pes, the
snake. "I have but a small clan of people. May we
not join your tribe?"

After consulting together for some time the five
clans agreed to allow the Snake clan to join them.

But the Bear said, "We will never call you a brother, for you have no feet with which to walk!"

"That will be all right," said the snake, "if we
may join your tribe."

And so the Bear clan, the Beaver clan, the Elk, the
Coyote, the Eagle, and the Snake clans journeyed am-
icably along together. But the Bear did not exchange
names with the Snake, as he had playfully done with
the chiefs of the other clans.

One summer day, when the plains lay blinking in

the sun and little cloud shadows went tiptoeing across
the hills, Higinee was out walking, alone. He had
just climbed a rather high hill, when he saw, at some
distance, a person who was much larger than anyone
he had ever seen.

He ran back to his brothers and cried, breathlessly,
"Oh, brothers! Beyond the tallest hill is another
brother; but he is much, much larger than even our
brother Elk! What shall we do?"

The Elk cried at once, "Let us kill him!"

"No!" objected the Beaver. "Why have we made
our Secret to Happiness? What is this Good Heart
Maker for? Let us take it and make peace with this
new brother!"

"The Beaver is right," approved the Bear chief.
"We will smoke together our Pipe of Peace, our Good
Heart Maker, our Secret to Happiness! Lead us to
this huge new brother, Higinee!"

So they all set out to meet the new brother.

But the big fellow was not friendly, and he shouted, crossly, "Get out of my world! The Great Spirit
created this earth for me, only. What are you doing
here?"

Hana called to him, "You are mistaken in thinking
this world belongs to you. It is ours, and you are de-
stroying our pastures, leaving nothing for our clans to
eat! Who are you, anyway?"

"I am the chief of the Buffalo clan," the big fellow
told them sullenly. "I thought this world was all mine,
but if it is meant for you, too, I suppose I must share
it with you."

"That is the right spirit!" said Hana. "Now let us smoke the Pipe of Peace together."

After lighting the Peace Pipe he blew the smoke to Todja-dowa, the four winds, then held it out to the buffalo. But the big fellow, still feeling disgruntled, refused to smoke the pipe with the other clans.

Then the Beaver said, "Brother Buffalo, we mean no harm to you or your people. Is it not better that we become fellow men and that there be peace, instead of quarreling, between us?"

"Yes," added the Elk, "and you will enjoy having us for your brothers, for we have a great power—the power to make fire. See?" The Elk made friction with his hoofs, and lighted a fire under a branch which the Beaver had cut off. Soon a cloud of smoke was rolling skyward.

The buffalo's eyes bulged in amazement. "Well!" he exclaimed. "I believe I would enjoy having such smart people for my brothers, after all. Hand me the Peace Pipe, and I will smoke with you!"

So the Bear lighted the pipe again, and, after first giving the smoke to the four winds, he handed the pipe to the Buffalo, who smoked it and then handed it to each of the other chiefs, in turn.

"Now I shall call you Wang-a-pee, Good Fellow," said the Bear.

"Then I shall call you Chaay-gee nea, Little Buffalo," replied the Buffalo. And he has done so to this day.

The Buffalo said, "Oh, brothers, you have the great power—fire. I, too, have a great power. I have Medicine Magic to heal the sick people of my clan. I can be the Medicine Man of our tribe, if you wish."

"That is good!" said the Bear. "You shall be the Medicine Man of our tribe. And now," he continued, "since we have seven clans in our tribe we are complete, for we are represented by a group of stars in the sky."*

"Seven is a good number," agreed Higinee, the youngest of the Bear clan. "Seven, and four, shall always be sacred numbers to us!"

"Because I was the first person to come out of the Waters and set foot on Mother Earth," stated Hana, "I am the head chief over all seven clans, and my clan is the head clan."

"That is good!" the other chiefs agreed.

And so Chief Hana told the chief of each clan what his special tribal duty was to be.

The Bear chief, always the general supervisor, would take over the entire management of the village, during the Summer Moons, he told his brother chiefs.

When rain was needed he would, through a long ritual of song prayer, entreat the Great Spirit to end the drouth. It has been the duty of the head chief, ever since that day, in the Beginning of our World, to bring rain to our thirsty land.

Hana told the Buffalo chief that he was to be the village manager during the fall season. He was to tell the people when to store their crops for winter, and he was to direct the people in a big celebration when the leaves began to put on their war paint.

---

* The constellation known as the Big Dipper.

At this celebration the Bear chief was to sing:*

I am very glad you come to us again, O Harvest.
We have been preparing for you.
May each day come peacefully to its sundown.
May our children always have the Great Spirit's strength!

Then the Buffalo chief was to sing:

Come, now, let us all be happy,
For we will harvest our grain
And prepare for the Snow Season.
We must never look back
To the day that is past,
But look to the day that comes.
There is Tomorrow . . .
And Tomorrow. . . .

The Buffalo chief was also to use his Medicine Magic to heal all the sick persons of the tribe.

The head chief told the Beaver chief that he was to be village manager during the winter—the Snow Season. He was to instruct the people how to make mud lodges, and to line them warmly. He was to show them how to dry meat and store it away.

The Elk chief was to be village manager during the three Spring Moons. He was to tell the people when to fertilize and plant their crops, and instruct them in the making of implements—the stone pick, and the hoe.

At the beginning of this season he was to hold a ceremony: After putting the pipe to the four winds he was to sing:

* These songs are literal translations of tribal songs of the Otoe.

> People of mine, listen,
> Listen to what I say!
> Let us take new courage,
> For the day has come
> That the warm sun shines on us again.
> Spring Morning is here;
> Our hard Winter Night is over!

He was to instruct the people to do their planting, after asking Wacunda's blessing.

When the seeds sprouted, the people were to be called together again to ask for another blessing from Wacunda. And again, when the first green vegetables were ready to eat.

The fourth ceremony was to be held when the roasting ears were ready. Then the Elk chief was to pray to Wacunda:

> Give us strength, through this food,
> That we may live to another day
> Of growing crops!

"The Coyote chief is to furnish the tribe with wisdom and cunning, and the Eagle chief is to bring hope and courage to those who need it," the head chief finished.

Then the Snake chief spoke. "Master," he said, "I, too, wish to have a share in the work. I, too, want to contribute toward the happiness of the tribe."

The Bear turned and looked at him.

"I will clear a place for the village," the Snake continued, "and will build a tepee for the head chief, in which to keep the sacred possessions of the tribe.

There the Peace Pipe, the Good Heart Maker, can be hidden."

"That is a good idea," said Hana.

And so a tepee was built for the head chief, and the other chiefs built their tepees around the head chief's tepee, to protect it, making it the center of a large circle.

The Elk chief built the first fire in the sacred tepee, and all seven chiefs gathered around it for their first big Council.

At the end of the story Sunlight looked up at his father, eagerly. "You are a descendant of Hana, aren't you, Father?"

"Yes, son. That is why I am chief of the Bear clan and head chief of our tribe today. At my death my oldest son will become head chief in my place."

Sunlight's chest expanded, ever so slightly, and his black eyes took on a new sheen. "I shall try to be a good one, Father, and a wise one, like you."

The rain, which had been tapping lightly on the sides of the tepee, began to pound down again with renewed vigor. The separate drops were like the beating of war drums, and the sudden wind was like the wailing of voices uplifted in a Scalp Dance song.

Circling Eagle put away her basketry and bent to straighten the robes of her bed. "Let us go to sleep now and forget the storm," she advised her family. "It is good to know that the thirsty prairie is getting a long, cool drink at last."

Before retiring the chief lifted the flap of the lodge door and, tilting back his head, he again thanked the Great Spirit for heeding his petitions.

Tilting back his head, he thanked the Great Spirit. . . .

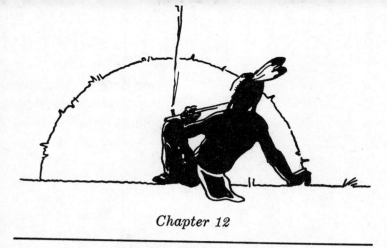

Chapter 12

THE BUFFALO HUNT

> O Buffalo. . . .
> Glad, glad you are,
> For the day of your roaming
> Has appeared again.
> May your little ones live
> As you live,
> Always.

So SANG Chief Mee-way-seh, Take-Blanket-Away, as he sat in front of his tepee sharpening his fine flint arrowheads.

The hunting season was here again. The head chief had been fasting with the Pipe Man four Suns and four Sleeps and had come out only this morning to face the Place of the Sunrise with prayers for the success of the hunt.

Now the Pipe Man stood in the door of the tepee of the head chief, ready to direct the hunt.

Sunlight. Spotted Tail, Surprise, and Sharp Claws

longed to go, too, but they were as yet too young. They decided to play "go hunting" at home.

"I shall be the Pipe Man," announced Sharp Claws, as he ran to the door of the tepee. "Now go that way, to the first hill," he directed, just as he had heard the Pipe Man

many times, "and that way, to the cottonwood tree by the stream, that way to the quarry, and that way to the wild-plum thicket." He gestured to Boo-wah-hoo, the east, to Bu-way-dee, the west, to Omayda, the north, and to O-lay-co-da, the south.

Chief Take-Blanket-Away looked up. "Do not forget to instruct your hunters to bring

They decided to play "go hunting" at home.

you and the chief the first game you kill," he reminded
his son, "for that is one of our fixed customs."

"Yes, you must bring me the first animal you shoot
with your bows and arrows," shouted Sharp Claws,
"for I am hungry after my long fast. Now, go! After
you have brought food for the chief and myself you
may go out on the prairie as far as you like, for it is
there you will find the herds of buffalo."

The boys had a good time playing at being grown
braves, and at night when their elders returned from
the chase they enjoyed hearing all the happenings of
the day. And how they looked forward to feasting
upon that fresh buffalo meat!

"Father, why do we so often say that man is superior to beast, when we speak of the buffalo?" asked
Sunlight, as he and his brothers were settling down
for the night.

"Is there a 'How' story about it?" asked Sharp
Claws.

"Yes, there is a 'How' story," replied their father
smilingly.

&

In the far-back times the buffaloes roamed over
the plains in one great herd. The two kinds of male
buffaloes—Chaay-gee, the Big Buffalo, and Loo-toe
Un-kee, One-Rib—fought many fierce battles over the
female buffaloes.

Sometimes a female buffalo would take the lead
over the herd and would persuade a few of the number
to wander away from the rest, until herd after herd

had left the one great herd and they could not all get back together again.

One of the smaller herds wandered close to an Indian village where lived a man and a woman and a small boy who was the woman's brother.

The man and woman were unkind to the boy. He was often hungry because they did not feed him all a growing boy should have.

One day when the lad was alone in the wigwam a woman with star fire in her eyes and a wind song on her lips came to the door and offered him food.

The next day she came, and the next, and each time she brought hunks of fresh venison, ripe berries, and little round corn-meal cakes.

On the fourth day the woman with star fire in her eyes and a wind song on her lips invited the boy to go home with her. Because he was very unhappy with his sister and her husband he decided to go.

The boy and the woman traveled many, many steps over smooth trails and rough trails, over grass-matted prairie and rocky knolls, until they came to a cliff on the side of a hill. In this cliff was a door through which the woman led the way to a deep cavern where the darkness of midnight dwelled.

When the boy's eyes became used to the darkness he saw that they were not alone in the cavern. Before them stood a herd of buffalo.

At first the lad's heart seemed to leap into his throat. There appeared to be as many buffaloes as there are fingers on a pine tree. But the woman with star fire in her eyes and a wind song in her throat told the boy the buffaloes were glad to see him and that they wanted him to be their leader.

She told him that she was, in reality, a buffalo, but that the Spirit of the Buffalo had given her the form of a human being.

The boy was complimented that they wanted him to be their leader. No one had ever seemed to think he mattered before; so he decided to stay.

The Spirit of the Buffalo helped him to become a strong and wise leader; and as he grew to manhood he taught the buffaloes many things. He also learned many things from the buffaloes.

When he became a man he married the woman with star fire in her eyes and a wind song on her lips; for the Spirit of the Buffalo had allowed her to remain as young as ever.

In the early Warm Moons they had twin sons whom the Buffalo Spirit changed into buffaloes. The Buffalo Spirit also changed the woman back into a buffalo.

"This will be but for a short time," he said, "so be patient until certain things are accomplished. I have spoken."

Now a very large buffalo desired to become the head chief of the buffalo tribe in the young man's place, and so the Buffalo Lady told him that he would have to prove his superiority.

She said to the man, "Tomorrow the herd will move to another grazing place. Chaay-gee, Big Buffalo, will persuade the herd to go while you are asleep, for I have heard his plans."

"I am listening," said the young man.

"If you will follow my instructions you will find us," the Buffalo Lady told him. "Go toward the Place of the Rising Sun until you come to a brier patch. From then on a bird will guide you."

When the young man awoke at dawn and found that the herd had left during the night he followed the Buffalo Lady's directions.

When he came to the brier patch a bird came and perched upon his shoulder. It proved to be one of his own sons whom the Spirit of the Buffalo had changed by means of his Medicine Magic.

The bird led him out of the brier patch. "Follow the buffalo tracks which are stained with red," twittered the bird, "for they are the tracks of your wife and sons."

The red tracks led him to the herd's new grazing place, where Big Buffalo, Chaay-gee, was standing

Chaay-gee was standing apart from the other buffaloes, bellowing to inform them that from then on he was going to be their leader.

apart from the other buffaloes, bellowing to inform them that from then on he was going to be their leader.

The Buffalo Lady was glad to see the young man, but she gave no sign of it. Later, when no one was listening, she said in a low voice, "Now you must do one thing more to prove your worthiness to remain leader of the buffalo herd: you must fight Chaay-gee. If you win, the Buffalo Spirit will change me back into a woman, and our sons will become human beings, too." The man was glad, for he wanted his wife of the star-fire eyes and the wind-song throat.

The prairie was pale with the dawn of day when the buffaloes of the herd gathered to watch the fight; and by the time the sun had risen from his lodge and started up over the rim of the prairie the big beast and the man had been tussling for some time without moving from the spot in which they had started.

It seemed as if the giant buffalo would surely rip the man to shreds with his knifelike horns or pound him to trail dust with his hoofs, but the man was as quick as Loo-glee, the Lightning, and the buffalo could not catch him unaware.

The sun was noon high and sending arrows of fire down upon the heads of the struggling man and beast, but they did not notice the heat.

Suddenly the man lost his footing. He slipped and fell in the dust with the horns of the buffalo coming down—down—down to gore him to death, when, with another lightning movement, the man grasped the horns of the buffalo and slowly forced his massive head away from him and into the dust of the ground.

A chorus of bellowing went up from the once silent crowd. The man's muscles were as hard as flint from his moons and many moons of training, and the buffalo could not raise his head. At last he bellowed, "It is enough! I have spoken."

"That is good," said the man, and he released the beast. "I have proved that man is superior to beast," he added, and no one disputed him.

Upon looking up again, the man saw the woman with star fire in her eyes and a wind song in her throat, and beside her stood two boys. The Buffalo Spirit had kept his promise to change them back into human beings.

"It is good!" said the man. "We will all be happy together."

And so they were, all through the Warm Moons and the Snow Seasons of their lives.

The chief finished his story with a smile. "That, my sons, is the answer to your question: 'Why do we so often say that man is superior to beast?' "

"The Evening Star is lighting the way for the Sleep Man," remarked Circling Eagle significantly.

"Yes, and there will be another big buffalo hunt for the tribe tomorrow," said the chief. "So we must all get plenty of rest tonight."

"And there will be another story tomorrow night?" asked Sharp Claws.

"Always, my son," rejoined their father, "for only in this manner can we preserve these precious legends for our coming generations."

During the following days the people of the Otoe village enjoyed feasts of fresh buffalo meat; and while the men were out on the hunt the women and children and the old men of the tribe stretched the buffalo skins upon large frames, for proper drying and curing.

These skins would later serve as rugs for the tepee floors, and would be painted with symbols in red, to represent the sun, stone, and forms of animals; blue, to represent the heavens, winds, water, and thunder; yellow, to represent sunshine.

Sunlight, Spotted Tail, Surprise, and Sharp Claws knew that on the buffalo hides for their own lodge would be painted the tracks of the bear, because their father was a chief of the Bear clan; there would be a symbol of the new moon, and of the sun. And, on winter evenings when he had plenty of time, Chief Take-Blanket-Away would take out his pots of dye and his brush and spend long hours painting scenes of the hunt, of days on the warpath, of many important events of his life.

Every night, because of the thrill of this season, the boys in the lodge of the head chief went to sleep with the Buffalo song on their lips and in their hearts.

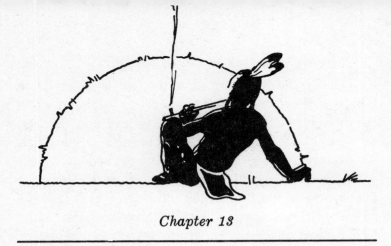

Chapter 13

HOW IT HAPPENS THE BADGER HAS CLAWS LIKE THOSE OF THE BEAR

THE CHIEF'S DEEP VOICE began a story at bedtime the next evening.

In the far-back times when animals could talk, Hay-jaay, the badger, lived with his family in a dark den in the side of a mountain.

He was a good provider, and there was always plenty of fresh meat for his squaw and little ones.

One day Mah-toe, the grizzly bear, came from his den across the ferny ravine to call upon the badger.

When Mah-toe saw how much food Hay-jaay had stored away in his den he asked for some to take home to Mrs. Bear and the cubs.

Hay-jaay was glad to give him some food, but when he came the next day, and again the next and demanded food the badger did not feel quite so glad.

Each time Mah-toe came he growled, "Old man, I

One day Mah-toe, the grizzly bear, came to call upon the badger.

am going to take some food back to my family, for
they have nothing to eat."

After many Suns had passed the bear decided to
move his family into a den near that of the badger so
he would not have to carry his supplies such a distance.

At first Hay-jaay was glad to have a new neigh-
bor, and he enjoyed watching the little badgers and
the bear cubs play together. But one day Mah-toe
pounced upon Hay-jaay, overpowering him and making him his slave.

He told Hay-jaay to clean the bear's den and to go
out every day for game for the bear family. This made
the members of the badger family sad at heart, for
they were not only humiliated but their stomachs were

often like hollow trees and their knees like quavering leaves because of the lack of food for themselves.

The bear always snatched all the game which the badger brought home, and gave him only the scraps after his wife and cubs had eaten all they could hold.

The bear cubs—that is, all but one—were sorry because of their father's brutal selfishness, and they often slipped something out to their little badger playmates.

The young badgers devoured every bite which the cubs gave them, because their stomachs were becoming more and more like hollow trees these days.

But one of the cubs was as much like his father as any little bear could possibly be. He always tried to keep his brothers from giving food to the hungry young badgers. He even ran and told his father, on one occasion, and Mah-toe was angry about it, so angry that he spanked the good little cubs with his heavy paw.

When Mr. and Mrs. Bear were away from their den one afternoon and all the cubs were out playing on the side of the mountain, one of the good little cubs slipped back and carried a big piece of meat over to the badger's den.

Mrs. Badger was very grateful for the meat, and she thanked the good cub for his kindness. "I'll save it for our supper," she said, as she put the meat in a crevice between two rocks where Mah-toe could not find it.

After awhile one of the little badgers who had been asleep awoke and asked for something to eat. His mother went to her hiding place and uncovered the meat; but what did she find? Not a piece of meat at all, but a *little baby boy!*

Mother Badger knew that it was a Token of Good for the badgers, and so she covered the baby with fur and anxiously awaited her husband's return.

Hay-jaay was very much interested when his wife told him about the baby boy.

"It is well!" he said. "We must take good care of the baby boy, and must never let Mah-toe know about him!"

Finally the boy was thigh high to a buffalo; then he became shoulder high to a buffalo, and soon he began to understand what a hard time the badgers were having.

Hay-jaay told him all about his troubles with Mah-toe and how cruel he was to the entire badger family.

The boy clamped his lips together and knotted his fists. "I will help you overpower the bear," he told Hay-jaay. "Wacunda put me here for your protection."

This made all the badgers feel lighthearted again.

"Go out and kill at least two deer and carry them to the hollow tree in front of the berrybushes," the boy instructed Hay-jaay. "I will be hiding there. Start butchering the one which will be lying nearest the bushes."

The badger did as he was told, and when the old brown bear came along, as they knew he would, he snarled, "Get away now. This game is mine!" But the badger did not pay any attention to him.

Mah-toe grabbed Hay-jaay and snarled threateningly. "What is the matter with you?" he demanded.

At that moment the boy stood up and shouted sternly, "I demand to know what you mean by such actions!"

Mah-toe jumped with fright, and immediately changed his tone to a polite one. He told the boy that he had been advising the badger to take the other deer, also.

The boy replied, "You are not telling me the truth! I warn you to leave the badger alone, hereafter!"

This made the bear furious, and he leaped at the boy and the badger, intending to kill them. But the boy was ready for this. With his bow and arrow he shot the bear and left his body beside the berrybushes. Then the boy and the badger carried the game back to the hungry badger family.

After they had feasted as they had not feasted for many moons and many moons the boy strode over to

With his bow and arrow the boy shot the bear.

Mah-toe's den and shot Mrs. Bear and the naughty cub. He let the good cubs live, but he cut the claws from the naughty cub's feet and gave them to the badger.

That is how it happens that all badgers, to this day, have claws like the bear.

"I like that story nearly as well as the one about how O-don-bah-shee, the bobcat, lost his tail," said Surprise, as his father finished.

"My favorite is how Mah-sjeem nea, the little white rabbit, got his pink eyes," said Spotted Tail.

"I like all the 'How' stories," said Sharp Claws. "Is there another one for tonight, Father?"

"Not tonight, my son," Chief Take-Blanket-Away replied. "See! The Evening Star has ridden far down the western sky toward her lodge. And if you will listen you can hear late sounds of the night—the Sleep song of the insects, the deep breathing of the wind in the cottonwoods. And somewhere out in the silver night Con-tha gah, the coyote, is again howling at the moon."

Chapter 14

PO-TOO YEO, THE SLEEP MAN

IN THE MOON WHEN THE ELK WHISTLE AT NIGHT, the trees began to put on their war paint and to do war dances with Todja-Omayda, the north wind.

Hoar frost lay heavy upon the buffalo grass every morning, and many birds, having lingered upon the prairie, were hastening on their journey to O-lay-co-da, the ever-warm country.

The song of this autumnal Moon was often upon the lips of the tribesmen now, for they knew a song for every moon.

> O elk, why do you whistle?
> The leaves are turning
> And we are ready for the fall,
> But I am glad your whistle has told me
> Ahead of time.

Sharp Claws often sang this song under his breath just as he was dropping off to sleep beneath his warm buffalo robes and after the Sleep Man tales of the evening were ended.

He could hear Tay-hah, Big-horn the elk, far out
on the prairie as he whistled for his mate; and from
somewhere in the starlit distance would come the
answer! Soon Tay-hah would be bounding across the
knolls and gullies, seeking the other whistler.

He could hear Tay-hah, the elk, as he whistled to his mate.

How Sharp Claws loved this month of September
—the romantic sounds of it, the crisp sweet smell of
it, the blazing color of it! October, the Moon When the
Wild Geese Fly South, would be much the same.

During the daytime Sunlight, Spotted Tail, Surprise, and Sharp Claws liked to hunt along the sun-
painted creeks for Toh-yun-neg, the bananalike paw-
paws which were ripe at that time, and they liked to
cut the plushy brown cattails in the swamp and
branches of red oak leaves and the yellow leaves of
the ash and the cottonwood trees along the river, to
decorate their new home—for Chief Take-Blanket-
Away and his helpers had lately finished building a
new winter lodge for the head chief and his family.

The builders had carefully constructed a framework of bent saplings, and covered it with sections of sod and clay—securing them with willow twigs. A buckskin "sail" was fastened above the chimney vent to guide the smoke from the lodge fire; and now, Circling Eagle was very busy lining the inside walls of the new lodge with buckskin hides which she had dressed and made smooth enough for the chief to paint his symbols upon while the family sat about the fire on winter evenings.

The Time of the First Snowfall had been set for a dedication ceremony for the new lodge, at which time all seven clans of their tribe would be invited in for feasting and dancing. The four sons of the chief had been talking of it all day, and were still talking of it now, as they strolled back along the trail toward the camp circle.

Sunlight and Spotted Tail had spent the afternoon gathering gourds to scoop out for drinking dippers and some to use for dance rattles by putting in pebbles after the gourds were properly cleaned out and dried.

Sharp Claws and Surprise had found some large gray seeds (known to white people as "Job's Tears") which they carefully gathered to take to their mother. They knew she would be delighted because she liked to string these seeds, along with tiny shells, or with elk teeth, to wear about her neck. She could never have too many beads!

When the boys reached home, at dusk, they saw their father sitting beside a brightly burning fire outside the lodge. As they came to his side they saw that he had just finished making a whistle from an eagle's wingbone, and was fastening, at the end, a bit of white down plucked from under the wing.

Sunlight bent to examine the whistle. "What does the downy white feather stand for, Father?" he asked.

The chief looked up, and in his intense black eyes was a look of pride in these sons who asked questions to further their knowledge.

"Sacred feathers are always white," he answered. "Many of our sacred articles are decorated with white feathers or white down. White stands for consecration—for all things pure."

"Is this whistle, then, a sacred article?" Sharp Claws asked, touching it respectfully.

"Yes, it is one of the seven articles for the sacred Pipe Dance rites, which are to be wrapped in a wildcat skin. Shall I show you the articles already wrapped in the skin?"

The boys were tense with excitement as they followed their father into the lodge and watched him unwrap the wildcat skin which lay among the sacred possessions guarded by the Pipe Man.

The boys knew that the chief had recently announced his intention to "Pipe Dance" members of the Ponca tribe which was encamped many, many steps—perhaps a journey of four Suns and four Sleeps away; that eight men had already asked to accompany him, and that only twelve would be allowed to go. They knew that these men and their father were getting together their gifts of bows and arrows, eagle war bonnets, otter skins, and buffalo robes to tie in bundles onto the backs of their ponies when the time came to start on their journey, and that their father himself was preparing the articles to be tied in the wildcat skin for the sacred rites of the Pipe Dance. Now, when they were about to see, with their own eyes, these sacred articles, the boys were at first too excited to speak.

Chief Take-Blanket-Away lifted from the wildcat skin two odd-looking pipes of about three feet in length and made of ash sapling. These pipes were without bowls, the stem of each pipe being thrust through the dried skin of a duck's neck which had the bill and feathers still on.

These pipes were decorated with eagle feathers and owl feathers, and with three clumps of tassels made from narrow strips of white fur taken from the breasts of rabbits. At the top of each tassel a red woodpecker head was bound to the pipestem. Balls of white down hung from buckskin thongs, and wherever the wood of the pipestem was not covered the chief had painted red and green stripes.

"These pipes," he said, "are the most necessary articles for the ceremony."

"Did you make them yourself, Father?" asked Spotted Tail.

"Yes. Only a man who has given many ponies, or has proved himself very brave, or has been a wise counsellor, may have the honor of making these pipes."

Next, the chief held up a red-painted crotched stick of hardwood. "In this crotch the mouthpieces of the two pipes are to rest," he said. Then he showed the boys two gourds, and a buffalo-bladder pouch filled with tobacco. All were painted with a green band about the middle, with a crossband dividing the design into four equal parts.

"Do you see these three feathers?" The chief pointed a big brown finger. "Two of these are for the pipe bearers, and one is for the runner who will announce our approach to the Ponca people. Later the feathers will be worn by others of the ceremony."

"Are these all of the articles that you are to provide, Father?" asked Surprise.

"Besides these there is to be a white ear of corn with a green stripe painted around the middle and with four stripes extending to the top of the ear. I must attend to that tomorrow," the chief replied. "And now let us lay this whistle upon the wildcat skin, with the feathered end toward the east, just as the mouthpieces of the pipes are laid."

After tying the wildcat-skin bundle and laying it carefully back the chief stood up and stretched himself. His tall form seemed to go up—up—up—like smoke toward the chimney vent.

"I think," he said, "that I smell baked pumpkin rings. The evening meal must be about ready."

"Yes," answered Circling Eagle, from over by the fire, "the meal is ready. And besides baked pumpkin rings we have little corncakes, wild honey, and the fruit of the prickly pear."

"Then we should sit down at once, for the men are coming this evening for a last rehearsal of the songs of the Pipe Dance," said the chief. "We start on our journey tomorrow."

As they were being seated Sharp Claws asked, "Why do the men of the Pipe Dance party always wear white blankets and paint their faces with white clay, for their journey?"

"So that any roving warriors of other tribes will allow them to ride on in peace," replied Chief Take-Blanket-Away. "To attack a Pipe Dance party would be to bring dishonor to the pipes."

Surprise swallowed a mouthful of corncake and honey before he asked his next question. "The Pipe Dance ceremony lasts several days, doesn't it, Father?"

"Yes, and it is a very important ceremony, my son."

"The Poncas will give you many ponies to bring home, won't they?"

"Yes, many ponies. Someday I will explain the entire ceremony to you boys, and teach it to you so that you may take part in it yourselves when you are grown. But now I must finish my meal so that I will be ready when the men come for rehearsal of the songs."

And so the boys asked no more questions that evening.

It was nearing the Time of the First Snowfall. Any day now might bring those first wavering white flakes, and Circling Eagle was feverishly preparing for the dedication ceremony of their new winter lodge.

Chief Take-Blanket-Away had returned from "Pipe Dancing" the Poncas, and had had much to tell his family about the Pipe Dance party's journey and visit among the Poncas.

This early evening he sat carving designs upon a new set of deer hoofs to be used as knee rattles for the coming celebration in his lodge. Occasionally he glanced at Circling Eagle, who made a pretty picture as she sat making a beautiful new robe to wear about her shoulders during the dedication ceremony.

The robe was of strips of rabbit fur which Circling Eagle was weaving together. Every other strip she placed with the fur out, and each end was finished with a tassel of white fur from the breasts of rabbits. She used sinew for thread, and her needle was a bone awl.

As she sewed the white tassels securely to the ends of the brown fur, first on one side of the robe and then on the other, she chanted, half under her breath, a little song about the "Dust-Trail" (the "Milky Way") which she had learned from visiting members of the Pawnee tribe:

> The prairie is dark
> But across the sky
> Is a trail of light.
> It is the ghost pathway
> Of the departed warriors.

The chief liked the music of her voice, but he had been noticing the darkness slinking about the doorway.

"Isn't it time to call our sons in from their play?" he suggested.

Circling Eagle arose. "Yes, it is growing late.

Already the Evening Star has lighted a pathway to our lodge."

She called from the doorway, "*Yah-wah shee-geh! Yah-wah shee-geh!*"

Her voice, as clear-toned as the village announcer's bell, ascended musically. "*Yah-wah shee-geh!*" she called again. "Do not linger at your star gazing, for you know that the moccasins of Po-too Yeo follow the trail of the Evening Star!"

The boys were sitting on the edge of the small knoll overlooking the village. Surprise had been pointing out the starry constellations he knew. "I have never yet seen that Sleep Man," he remarked a bit crossly.

"Nor I," answered Sunlight, "and I have often tried to keep awake so that I could catch sight of him."

"I wonder how he looks," Surprise said dreamily. "He must be very, very aged, for he has been putting children to sleep for generations and generations."

Surprise had been pointing out the starry constellations.

"I picture him as a very *tall* man," offered Sharp Claws, "and he slips along like a big shadow. His headdress is long and full of large eagle feathers which flutter across our eyes as he bends over us. I believe that is the reason we can never see his face."

"But his face must be kind," Surprise said as the four arose to go in, "for although I do not like his coming to put us to sleep I think only a nice man would put such good bedtime stories into the mouths of our parents and into the mouths of the tribe's old-men storytellers."

"Father," said Sharp Claws as he and his brothers settled down beside the lodge fire, "how do you know that Po-too Yeo comes to put us to sleep? Have you ever seen him?"

"How do I know that there are Water Spirits and Tree Spirits?" responded Chief Take-Blanket-Away. "And how do I know there is a Thunder Bird? I hear him but I do not see him. I hear the Water Spirits and the Tree Spirits talking, but I do not see them!"

"Yes," agreed Sharp Claws, "we do believe there are Water Spirits and Tree Spirits and that there is a Thunder Bird, because we hear them. But we do not hear the Sleep Man."

"Ah, but we go to sleep, do we not?" interrupted the chief. "And we find ourselves in the Faraway Place of Dreams. Could anyone other than a Sleep Spirit take us there?"

"Po-too Yeo is a Sleep Spirit," he continued. "He moves silently and as mysteriously as do other spirits.

"No one has ever seen his face; no one has ever heard his movements; but everyone has felt his magic touch. When our eyelids feel as if they were weighted with stones, then it is we know that Po-too Yeo has us under his spell!

"His moccasins follow the trail of the Evening Star, as your mother often tells you, and he slips from lodge to lodge, stirring no dust at all, and puts into the mouths of grown people the bedtime stories you hear night after night.

"That is why we call the stories Sleep Man tales, as you know. After the Sleep Man tales are over—sometimes during the telling of them—Po-too Yeo mixes his sleep medicine for the young.

"There, I have told you all I know about this Sleep Spirit. It is all anyone knows about him. You may tell your own children, someday—and your children's children—when they ask you as all children do: 'How do you know that Po-too Yeo comes to put us to sleep?' "

When Chief Take-Blanket-Away had finished speaking he sat for a long time, puffing at his pipe and gazing into the lodge fire. Perhaps he saw, in the fluttering flames, pictures of his own childhood, or perhaps he was visioning the future days when he might be telling these same Sleep Man tales to his grandchildren.

At any rate, when he lifted his eyes again he observed, with a smile, that Po-too Yeo had made his invisible, stealthy entrance, and had woven his nightly spell over the four play-weary boys on the opposite side of the fire, while the cold moonlight nestled, like snow, upon the quiet lodges of the village.

"Sleep, my sons," he said, "and may the Great Spirit bring sunrise to your hearts!"